# CREATIVE
# PROCRAS-
# TINATION

# CREATIVE PROCRAS-TINATION

Organizing Your Own Life

*Frieda Porat, Ph.D.*

HARPER & ROW, PUBLISHERS

SAN FRANCISCO

Cambridge
Hagerstown
Philadelphia
New York

1817

London
Mexico City
São Paulo
Sydney

FIRST EDITION

*Designed by Jim Mennick*

---

**Library of Congress Cataloging in Publication Data**

Porat, Frieda, 1925–
    CREATIVE PROCRASTINATION.

   1. Time allocation—United States. 2. Procrastination—Psychological aspects. 3. Self-realization. 4. Job stress. I. Title.
HN90.T5P67   1980      158'.1       80–7750
ISBN 0–06–250690–0

---

81  82  83  84  10  9  8  7  6  5  4  3

# Contents

# Acknowledgments

Thanks are due to Henry Still for his invaluable help in the writing and editing of this book and to Clayton E. Carlson, Publisher, Harper & Row, San Francisco, for his constructive advice and assistance so generously given.

# Introduction

Many books have been written about time management, ranging from practical how-to-do-it instructions to books designed for specific audiences such as business executives. What I find missing in all of them is the psychological and human aspect of time management: paying attention to ourselves, being aware of our bodies, our needs, and our physical and mental limitations and feelings.

The primary element overlooked in most previous works on this subject is the technique for balancing work effectiveness and productivity with maintenance of a high quality of life. Time management in this context must include attention to health, more relaxation and creativity, stress reduction, and more joy in our everyday life. It also includes scheduled time for planning, thinking and creative procrastination.

We have viewed time management from the vantage point of the efficiency expert for too long. This perspective is rooted in the work ethic and time-and-motion studies which, in their proper time and place, have contributed to the productivity of men and women in all occupations. High levels of efficiency, however, should not require that every hour of the day be filled with activity and motion. Indeed, one problem in American commerce, industry, and corporate endeavor, is that we are so busy with the present that we do not leave time to plan the future. We do not take the time to clarify—on *our* life scale—what is really important.

We are so busy being busy that we are ruled by time instead of controlling its use to our greater good. The average business executive, for example, spends most of the day responding to external demands by superiors, subordinates, customers, or vendors. He feels guilty if he sits back for a while to plan future actions or indulge in free-form thinking, because he has been programmed against appearing idle. The only time he can feel comfortable using discretionary time, *in any way he chooses,* is when every other demand has been satisfied. Such moments are rare in today's business environment.

We are so conditioned to use every minute of the day "wisely" that even when we are tired and don't feel well, we push ourselves to do more in order to justify our existence or our paycheck. Working in this manner leads to stress— and *dis*tress—because of the unnatural tension between the working part of us that is going through the job motions, and the whole person who should be engaged in getting the work done comfortably and enjoyably.

There is an inescapable interdependence between managing time and paying attention to overall well-being. Helping you to achieve this balance—whether you are the chairman of the board, a middle-level executive, or a beauty shop operator—is the key of this book. That balance, once you have it, will improve the productivity and integrity of your life.

Central to shaping a balanced life is the ability to distinguish between negative and positive procrastination, and eliminating the causes of negative procrastination from your life.

I visualize negative procrastination as those idle and unplanned uses of time which block us from achieving a more fulfilled life. Positive or creative procrastination, on the other hand, denotes time that is deliberately *planned and scheduled* for your own use.

I recommend scheduling discretionary time to think, to meditate, to collect information, and to be creative. In learning to overcome drifting, negative procrastination, the hours of discretionary time will be filled with greater satisfaction and lead to more meaningful productivity.

As I examine methods for making more creative use of time I also will consider the stress that often occurs in managerial positions, how to avoid the pressure that leads to distress, and how to convert stress into greater power and motivation.

Time is our most important resource; we all have it in an equal measure. The only question is how to control it intelligently for our benefit, profit, and to enhance our lives. If we pay attention to the human aspects of time management, we will not become robots or machines. Rather we become freer people, people who control the previously uncontrolled spirals of life that build tension, inhibition, and frustration.

We take charge of our own life.

We take responsibility for the way we use time.

We control time to serve our own needs and to achieve healthier, fuller lives.

We add joy and health to our lives through creative procrastination.

Time management, in this view, incorporates needs we may have for creative day-dreaming, relaxation, and play. At the same time, we can have important goals along with the power, stamina, and energy to fulfill them. No energy will be wasted on depression, anxiety, or indecision. This can only be achieved through using time for the greatest benefit of the whole person.

# 1

# Creative Procrastination

*What is creative procrastination?*

In order to plant the concept firmly in your mind from the beginning, carefully read the following two definitions, thinking of the first as *negative* and the second as *positive*.

The dictionary definition of procrastination:

> *To put off intentionally, habitually, and reprehensibly the doing of something that should be done; delay attending to something until some later time.*

The second (new) definition which will help you to use yourself as a whole person:

> *Creative (or positive) procrastination is the planned and deliberate gift of prime time to yourself each day to do what gives you greatest satisfaction, including not doing anything, if that is your choice.*

The difference between these two definitions is the core of this book. Note that the first definition of procrastination contains three major elements: we put off performing a

1

duty *intentionally;* we do it *habitually;* and we do it *reprehensibly.* The last of the three is the most powerful element governing our attitudes toward using time. It is "evil," "sinful," "reprehensible," to waste time. Certainly, if time is truly wasted, there is no argument about the "wrongness" of it. However, the usual choice which must be made is between using time to fulfill requirements and using it to promote greater harmony of thought and action within ourselves or within our relationships with others.

We suffer from anxiety and guilt when we put off until later—or never—what we should do today. From a heritage salted with aphorisms by Benjamin Franklin and other wise ancestors, we learn: "Never put off until tomorrow what you can do today," "Early to bed and early to rise makes a man healthy, wealthy, and wise," and "Waste not time while time shall last, for after death 'tis ever past."

From earliest memory we are taught to believe that postponing a task is bad, *per se.* We label ourselves as lazy, irresponsible, disorganized. These judgments were drummed into us by parents and teachers who were themselves imbued with the dictum that hard, uninterrupted work is the only pathway to happiness and success. As a result, most of us labor under the conviction that, during our working years, time must not be wasted. Later, perhaps, we will have earned a rest in retirement. The average person, executive as well as subordinate, works at least eight hours a day at a factory or office, stopping only during designated minutes for coffee or lunch, and then is admired for industriousness in carrying work home.

But despite this indoctrination, all of us do procrastinate at one time or another, and then feel guilty about it.

Negative procrastination usually stems from fear of a task, distaste, or disinterestedness. Obviously, putting off a task because we don't like it only intensifies the anxiety and guilt which result from failing to perform. Once it is begun, negative procrastination may become a habit and a serious impediment to achieving life goals.

For example, Charles is a young middle-management executive in a large manufacturing firm. For the first time he has his own private office and, along with his new job, he inherited an experienced secretary.

She begins the morning by categorizing mail and memos and placing them so they will be Charles's first confrontation of the day. Although he knows that personal contact with the foremen and other workers on the assembly line is a prime requisite of his supervisory position, Charles finds it easier to browse through his correspondence and policy directives, most of which do not require immediate attention. He hesitates to admit it, but Charles is reluctant to make his rounds of the factory floor because his old buddies may ridicule him in his new exalted position.

Thus, routine and habitual matters absorb Charles's morning hours every day. These are hours which should be creative and productive, but he allows them to slip away without accomplishing the priorities of his job.

Charles can break his negative procrastination patterns, or he can allow them to become habitual until he is reminded by a superior that he isn't performing his job very well. He won't feel in harmony with himself and his environment until he changes his work habits.

## The Creative Way

Since everyone will procrastinate now and then, it is possible to schedule free time and use it creatively, while at the same time accomplishing essential work. This is the point of the second definition of creative procrastination.

Under the old definition, time is stolen and (because of guilt feelings associated with it) can't be used for complete pleasure and relaxation. The difference, in essence, is the difference between killing time and making it live for you. In creative procrastination, you give prime time to yourself while fully considering what must be done each day and allowing adequate time to do it. The distinction lies in realistic planning and the discipline to follow through.

You may find it difficult to accept the concept of creative procrastination because you have been taught to make "wise" use of every moment. The wisest use of some of your time may actually be that devoted to planning, reflecting, organizing your thoughts, or just relaxing. You may have trouble believing that you do need and deserve time for yourself in order to become a more effective human being. As stated by the French sociologist Jacques Ellul:

> The man or woman of the technical world has effectively suppressed the respite of time indispensable to the rhythm of life; between desire and the satisfaction of desire there is no longer the duration which is necessary to real choice and examination.
>
> There is no longer respite for reflecting or choosing or adapting oneself, or for acting or wishing, or pulling oneself together. The rule of life is; no sooner said than done. Life has become a race course composed of instantaneous variations of the universe, a succession of objective events which drag us along and lead us astray without anywhere affording us the possibility of standing apart, taking stock and ceasing to act.*

In our hyperactive society, everyone needs time for "standing apart, taking stock and ceasing to act." Every person needs and deserves time alone, time to be used as desired, and everyone can achieve this without guilt or anxiety while fully performing the important tasks of life. It is time we must have if we are to maintain good mental health,

---

*Jacques Ellul, *The Technological Society* (New York: Alfred A. Knopf, 1964), p. 329.

increase our productivity, and create a harmonic balance between work and play.

Before examining in detail how we can take responsibility for, and control of, our use of time, we need to see more clearly how we developed our ideas of time. How and why did the work ethic gain mastery and power over our need to live a balanced life according to natural rhythms and abilities?

## The Work Ethic

One axiom states that hard work made America great. To a degree that may be true, but in our accomplishment-oriented culture we often drive ourselves to succeed without a clear definition of what we mean by success. Most of us lead busy, stressful lives without leaving time for relaxed self-indulgence. We try to emulate the American ideal of the self-made millionaire, attaining an ever higher material standard of living.

We are now beginning to realize that we are on a treadmill in the home, factory, store, or office. Few of us take the time to examine our abilities, our natures, and our needs for leisure, to see if we are living as we can and should. We seldom take an hour to think and create, an hour which might be the most valuable time of all.

Where did the so-called work ethic originate? The phrase conjures an image of sweaty, dusty men laboring on farms or in the steel mill, of women with hands red from washing clothes or hoeing gardens, their bodies misshapen from repeated child bearing. The work ethic took form in those years when long, hard physical labor was necessary for basic physical survival.

Later, water- and coal-driven machines began providing some of the energy previously drained from human bodies. The six-day work week was shortened to five, and by 1960 the average work week was 38.5 hours. (Since that time there has been a gradual but spotty tendency toward a four-day work week, but in most cases where this has been attempted, the week consists of four ten-hour work days.) Farm tractors replaced horses performing more and tireless work. Electricity powered the factories, and housework drudgery was eased by vacuum cleaners, motorized washing machines, and automatic dish washers.

Machines created dramatic gains in human productivity. Fewer hours of *necessary* work were required but the work ethic lingered on, driving men and women to seek more of the world's luxury goods after their basic needs had been satisfied.

One man, who grew up on a Midwestern farm during the depression years of the 1930s, remembers his father's obsession with early rising, a habit he equated with virtue, hard work, and success. Each morning, the father would stand in the pre-dawn darkness at the foot of the stairs and shout: "All right! Everybody out. Time to rise and shine." If mother and sons and daughters were not downstairs within minutes, he would physically pull the youngsters out of bed.

That was this man's clearest memory of his father—being rudely roused from sleep and hustled off to farm chores before the sun was up, especially in the cold of winter.

As the father grew older, his capacity for work diminished, but he never lost his obsession for early rising. After he sold his farm, the father continued to get up at dawn even though there was nothing for him to do. Fortunately, the work habit does not always lead to the same excesses, but in his case, in the senility of his 80s, he would get up as early as 3 A.M. and wander aimlessly around the house, in some corner of his mind still living the ethic of never wasting a moment.

## Why We Procrastinate Negatively

For many of us, work is not the joy it should be and, accordingly, we procrastinate negatively even though we feel guilty when we do. Others of us are stopped from completing assignments because of one or more of the inner fears listed below. As an exercise, try to identify those fears that prevent you from beginning or completing a job at optimum speed. Rate yourself on each item; zero indicates no fear and five designates severe anxiety. You will thus discover which barriers you must overcome in your effort to avoid procrastinating negatively:

1. Fear of disapproval
2. Fear of failure
3. Fear of making a mistake
4. Fear of an undesirable outcome
5. Fear of being wrong
6. Fear of sticking your neck out
7. Fear of rocking the boat
8. Fear of being alone in your struggle
9. Fear of being noticed
10. Fear of *not* being noticed
11. Fear of confronting the unknown
12. Fear of ambiguous situations
13. Fear of accepting responsibility
14. Fear of committing yourself
15. Fear of getting into trouble
16. Fear of unexpected situations
17. Fear of too difficult a task
18. Fear of being less than perfect
19. Fear of exposing your inadequacies
20. Fear of being rejected
21. Fear of being on the wrong side
22. Fear of being embarrassed

23. Fear of approaching other people
24. Fear of having your efforts criticized
25. Fear of confronting the situation

If you have scored four or five on a number of the above fears, you know you suffer from attitudes leading to negative procrastination. If most of your answers are zero or one, you are ready for the positive use of discretionary time.

In addition to fear, there are five other problem areas which encourage negative procrastination. These are: people, habits, emotions, motivation, and attitude.

In each of the problem areas, as set out below, rate yourself again on a scale of zero to five, zero indicating no problem and five showing a severe problem:

*People problems*
- Discomfort with high-level managers, top customers, etc.
- Reluctance to give others bad news
- Avoidance of those who might prove difficult or critical
- Uncertainty about what others expect of you
- Reluctance to work with others
- Hiding feelings from others
- Violent expression of anger

*Habit problems*
- Disorganized work habits
- Restlessness and inability to concentrate
- Daydreaming
- Slow response to direction

*Emotional problems*
- Feeling guilty after not reacting promptly to a demand or situation
- Bouts of depression

– Worry and anxiety
– Low tolerance to frustration
– Panicking or freezing under pressure
– Reluctance to bring attention to oneself

*Motivation problems*
– Uneasiness about accepting responsibility
– Reluctance to commit oneself or become involved
– Lack of self-confidence
– Low enthusiasm about job
– Unwillingness to take a chance

*Attitude problems*
– Tendency to adopt a negative attitude
– Reluctance to make decisions
– Boredom
– Feeling work is not worthwhile
– Dissatisfaction with superiors and/or associates
– Dissatisfaction with salary level

The purpose of the preceding exercises was to increase your self-awareness and set the stage for change.


## Reversing Attitudes

Now it's time to begin turning attitudes and behavior around so that the time you take for yourself adds to the quality of life. Some of the ground rules:

- Be aware of your body.
- Know your capabilities, your intellect, your creativity and your emotions. Let these guide you in using time.
- Leave prime time for yourself each day.
- Concentrate upon inner rather than outer needs.
- Don't feel guilty about stopping when you're tired.

If you are typical, your workday morning begins with hastily-gulped orange juice and coffee, a glance at the morning headlines, and a dash out the front door. The rest of the day is "owned" by your employer, your clients, your patients, your customers—everyone but you.

Whatever your occupation, if you do not deliberately set aside some private time, you're probably spending ninety-five percent of your day on other things and other people. Your proportion of work and leisure is seriously out of balance. The concept of balance leads to the question of what motivates us to be more efficient and productive.

## Motivation

Everyone seeks two kinds of rewards, internal and external. The former includes those things you give yourself: pride, self-respect, self-esteem, and the awareness that you are a winner capable of achieving whatever is important. External rewards certainly include money and power, but even greater than that can be the esteem of others, those who say:

"I'm proud of you, you did a good job."

"Your new office has carpeting and a corner window."

"You're invited to join . . ."

Our desire for both internal and external laurels is linked with life goals.

Have you examined your goals lately? Have your needs and desires changed since you were young? Is it possible to achieve your goals (and your rewards) by working fewer hours, but working them more wisely?

Examine your motives for struggling each year to increase your income. Are you gaining what you want, or are you increasing the amount of time you work only to pay more taxes? If a high income gives you sufficient emotional compensation in pride and prestige, that's fine, but if you're giving a large portion of your work time to the government, it might be more satisfying to choose your own charity. We tend to be slaves to the formula that hard work plus income equal pleasure, but perhaps if we gave some of those hours to ourselves while accepting a smaller income, we might experience greater pleasure and satisfaction. It's time to rethink the equation.

## The Good Life

All of our efforts are geared toward the ultimate goal of a "good" life. What constitutes the good life is up to you, including the decision to live it as you go along or postpone it to some indefinite future when you believe your work will be finished and you can *then* relax and enjoy.

Most people plan their education and work, but not their leisure, play, or social life. One might schedule a vacation (and work hard at playing) but then ignore time for pleasure and relaxation the rest of the year. We need some prime time for ourselves every day, and we need to learn how to enjoy it without feeling guilty.

First, accept the fact that no one can be active every waking moment. Your day contains certain hours of productive energy and others that are nonproductive. In accepting this reality you grant yourself permission to organize time according to your values, needs, and moods. There is a creative element:

- It is your privilege and responsibility to make these daily and hourly choices and implement them.
- You cannot blame others or complain about a lack of time to do what you wish.
- You are responsible for selecting the time use choices that bring pleasure and self-renewal into your day.

The only real question is whether you have the courage, perseverence, and willpower to take and keep control of time rather than permitting it to control you.

One person may say: "Once I let myself procrastinate, I just drift and daydream. I never get back to finishing my work."

Or: "I never get started in the first place. If the job looks hard or boring, I eat instead—cup cakes, candy bars. For me, procrastination means eating and gaining weight."

Another person says: "I know myself. When I get bogged down in the middle of a job, I call a friend or read a magazine. That's more fun than work, so I don't dare let myself procrastinate."

Some people hesitate to begin work because they can't distinguish between what is essential and what is trivial—a true waste of time.

It's sad to hear someone say: "My life has been wasted." The statement means that this person *cannot remember* significant things he or she did during free time. This is typical of people who procrastinate negatively. To avoid this feeling of emptiness, you must identify activities that are satisfying and fulfilling, and then incorporate them into a daily time structure. If you fail to do this, your life is chaotic and unplanned, and positive change seems impossible to achieve. Because you don't know what you want, you cannot be motivated to act and change your life.

One inner voice is countermanded by another: "Tomorrow I could set the alarm half an hour earlier than usual and have that time to exercise or read while the house is quiet. Or I can sleep late because I don't have to be in the office tomorrow morning."

Willpower is essential for using planned free time successfully. One way to build it is through self-affirmation. Before you fall asleep at night, quietly make short affirmative statements such as:

"I'll wake up at 6:30 A.M. I will jog for 20 minutes. My rewards will be energy, self-discipline, and good health. *I will do it.*" And you can if you want to.

## Overcoming Guilt

Guilt is a companion to the anxiety which sets in after you have taken time for yourself but failed to use it for your benefit. You may be the type of person who feels guilty because you think you don't deserve pleasure, that you're not productive enough to earn it. To counteract that kind of guilt, repeat to yourself each day: "I deserve pleasure in my life. I deserve fun. I deserve a good balance of work and play."

Guilt is the dominant feeling suffered by people who do not manage time and tasks effectively. To overcome guilt, you must take control of your structured work time, as well as the time you choose for creative procrastination. Analyze your work pattern:

- Is it difficult for you to begin a project, or to keep it going?
- How frequently do you need to pause for a rest?
- Do you fritter away time rearranging papers on your desk?

Don't delay beginning a task because it doesn't challenge you. Begin. Finish. Then bask in your earned free time. If a job is complicated, capitalize on a knowledge of your work habits. If you believe you can finish a task in five hours, allocate six and enjoy your hour of creative time early in the day.

Some people get bogged down in the middle of a project. If this is your pattern, begin the assignment early and concentrate. Later, when you are stuck and feel dull, take your free time without guilt. Walk the dog, jump rope, meditate, find a peaceful place away from your co-workers. Then come back to your project refreshed, and finish it.

The more intense the work, the more you need to release built-up tensions. A change of pace and path are necessary for creative productivity. You can either enjoy a pleasure break or feel guilty about it. Since rest is essential, learn to enjoy it. Plan when you are going to take your deserved break for creative procrastination, and then use it according to plan.

## Eliminating the Negative

You may use your free time for anything that gives you satisfaction—including nothing. Be careful, however, not to slip back over the line into negative procrastination and its accompanying depression, pain, and emotional paralysis. Be aware of the difference constantly.

Warren, for example, deals with difficult clients and a demanding boss at the office. He comes home feeling frustrated and exhausted. He doesn't want to talk about problems and doesn't want to hear about the family's. He is surly to his wife and children. He has a beer before dinner, several more afterward and then watches television until he falls asleep on the couch.

This is his free-time pattern day after day, but it is *not* positive or creative. It is escape from purposeful living. Indeed, much of the evasive behavior we associate with procrastination is actually an effort to escape the pain of life.

Frank's assignment is to prepare a proposed budget for his department. He dreads beginning it because he fears his associates will not take the time to provide necessary information. He also believes he doesn't have enough time to do it.

Since he doesn't know how to resolve his problem, Frank slides around it by finding other ways to look busy. He makes unnecessary phone calls, writes low priority letters and lower priority memos. Instead of directly asking others for their input to the budget, he writes memos to them.

Meanwhile, the unstarted assignment looms menacingly. Frank's anxiety grows as the deadline draws nearer, placing him under a stress that is dangerous to his health.

Obviously, this is negative procrastination. Frank can solve his problem two ways:

- By persistently seeking out the information he needs and dividing the job into small steps to be completed in sequence.
- By asking for more time and using it for necessary research and analysis.

Here are other examples of negative procrastination:

- Spending high amounts of energy on low-priority jobs, such as answering routine correspondence instead of planning future work.
- Reading the paper instead of writing a job resumé.
- Staying in the same dead-end job because it's safe and familiar.
- Failing to seek information about school or job because once obtained, the information would have to be acted on.
- Delaying the start of a diet or exercise program until next Monday.
- Clinging to a damaging personal relationship. (It's simpler to be a victim than risk changing your life.)
- Avoiding learning a new sport or skill because of fear of failure. (If you don't try, you'll never know.)
- Refusing to confront your addiction to alcohol, drugs or tobacco.
- Neglecting to write a will because it's a reminder of mortality.
- Putting off a necessary confrontation with your boss, a friend, husband, or wife because "things will work themselves out."

- Refusing to work on tax returns until the last minute because you're angry with the government.

Negative procrastination is the tendency to always say: "I'll do it later." But *later* never comes and life slips away in a blur of half-completed or never-started projects. Your self-confidence seeps away and you despise yourself for your weakness. This leads to depression and lethargy that prevent positive change.

Learning to like yourself and believing that you deserve to include self-satisfaction and relaxation as well as work in your schedule is, therefore, the first step toward creative procrastination.

## Building Self-Esteem

Fears that block you from achieving what you want and need are rooted in low self-esteem and lack of confidence. The following are some basic steps to help build, or rebuild, your self-esteem.

1. Realize that only *you* can give self-esteem to yourself. If you depend upon others for your sense of worth, you will always be vulnerable to despair.
2. Tell yourself: I deserve pleasure, I deserve time to develop my personal interests. Believe it. Act on it.
3. Write down what you will do tomorrow—at what hour —for relaxation and pleasure.
4. Clarify your values. What are your priorities? What comes first in your life? Do you spend your time in accordance with these priorities?
5. Be prepared to pay the price for control of your time. Every decision is a coin with a "yes" and "no" side. If you choose to play tennis twice a week, you no longer have those time slots available for reading,

planning, or building a garden wall. Decide which activity is most important.

6. Listen to the different parts of yourself. If you feel divided or drained of energy, you may be internally divided about using time. Your student self may need time to finish a term paper but your "inner child" wants to go to the movies. Decide who gets the action and focus your energy.

7. Relinquish past self-images that diminish you now. Perhaps parents, friends, or teachers labeled you when you were too young to fight back and you incorporated their judgments into your self-image. Just because you were once called fat, plain, unpopular, or slow to learn, does not mean that you must wear those negative labels for life. Give yourself credit for every positive change you've made and every one you're attempting. Bring your self-image up to date.

8. Think positively. We were taught not to boast but that does not mean we should denigrate ourselves. We can recite our faults all too easily. Give yourself reassurance and kindness. Don't put up with those who put you down.

9. Present yourself the gift of creative procrastination each day. Cherish the time for pleasure, planning, productivity, and mental health. Don't say, *I'm too busy*. The busier you are the more you need free time to remain in balance.

10. Take satisfaction in small achievements, especially actions that others may not know are difficult for you. Praise yourself when you are able to confront an imposing authority figure or audience, when you project friendliness despite natural shyness, or when you learn a new skill.

11. *Don't give up*. Building self-esteem is the work of a lifetime. Some days you will suffer setbacks; negative

inner voices will be strong. Continue to affirm your self-worth. Learning to like yourself takes persistence and patience.

Scheduling free time for creative and recuperative purposes is the highest order of importance. It will become an accepted part of your life as you become aware of your capabilities and limitations. You will learn to focus upon internal needs rather than those dictated by others. By freeing blocks of time for yourself, you will find productivity and effectiveness increasing in those time portions given over to others and to work.

# 2

# Holistic Time Management

Time management is an integral part of any program designed to keep your body and mind in prime operating condition. In gaining control of free time you are rewarded with a general feeling of well-being and confidence. This is a sensation few people experience in their daily struggle to cope with work, solve problems, and manage stress.

We are familiar with the terms *dis*-comfort and *dis*-ease, but we usually don't think about their opposites—comfort and ease. Definitions of illness permeate the medical books, but rarely do we see an attempt to define total wellness. We recognize wellness only as the absence of sickness, but not that the opposite is also true. We should all be experiencing the vibrant stimulation that comes when our minds and bodies are healthy and functioning together toward a peak of creative endeavor—working easily, comfortably, productively.

Unfortunately, most people abdicate responsibility for good health. Because of penicillin and a plethora of so-

19

called miracle drugs and diagnostic tools developed or discovered during the past generation, we have delivered ourselves over to the doctor. We follow a hectic and careless pace, assuming that if anything goes wrong with our body the doctor will fix it. If we suffer a cold, headache, or insomnia, we reach for a pill. Despite the stress of living, we stubbornly continue our old life-style—including destructive personal habits—without seeing the long-term conditions that contribute to our discomfort.

Thousands of relatively young men and women are stricken by heart disease, stroke, digestive disturbances, organ failure, and cancer. Often these people are the high achievers who push themselves to greater efforts without learning how to manage stress or express feelings. This person does not resolve stressful situations until overcome by them.

## Taking Responsibility

Just as we learn to take control of time, we must also take responsibility for our lives. For our overall mental and physical health, we need to take charge of all the things necessary to maintain our bodies in top condition. We should think of our *own* health care instead of relying upon sickness care, which is the primary function of medical science today. When we go to the physician to be cured, we are only given medication or surgery to ease the symptoms. The damage usually is already done.

However, if you control use of time, and use the hours you gain to pay closer attention to your health, then you increase the odds for living and working more comfortably and productively. Those extra minutes you've earned for yourself each day may be used for walking, exercising, relaxing, or for planning and following a better diet.

Here are major elements to consider as you take time to listen to your body's needs:

- Adequate exercise
- Proper nutrition
- Relaxation
- Changing your life-style—eliminating unhealthy habits and taking responsibility for how you live

You may take your present behavior and condition for granted, feeling your performance to be adequate in each category. That may also indicate, however, that you don't know how well you *could* feel if you changed your attitudes and behavior.

## Physical Fitness

Answering the following questions can help you rate yourself in terms of overall health.* Write your answers on a separate sheet of paper along with any comments you may wish to make. No one else need see your answers unless you choose to reveal them:

1. Do you now weigh considerably more than you did when younger?
2. Are you proud of your body when you look at yourself nude in a full-length mirror?
3. Do you exercise at least thirty minutes nearly every day, enough to increase your heart and breathing rate substantially?
4. Do you include slow stretching exercises in your routine every day?
5. Do you make time for exercise even when other activities seem more important?

---

*Paraphrased in part from Donald B. Ardell, *High Level Wellness: An Alternative to Doctors, Drugs and Disease* (Emmaus, Pa.: Rodale Press, 1977).

6. Do you belong to a health club or other fitness-oriented organization?
7. Does your company provide or encourage exercise programs for its employees?
8. Do you understand the ways in which physical exercise and fitness benefit your body?

How you "scored" on this first series of questions should be self-evident not only in terms of what you are doing or not doing, but also in your *attitudes* about physical fitness. Many people are defensive because they do not like to admit that they lack the self-discipline to improve.

You can't take a pill to firm up a flabby belly or muscles. Nor can you take medicine to improve the poor posture that cramps internal organs, to deepen breathing that improves the oxygen supply to your tissues, or to work the heart to increase its strength and blood circulation. Physical exercise *can* do those things but most people are not active enough to keep their bodies in shape.

If you find it uncomfortable to confront these physical fitness questions, it may help to think of them in relation to someone else, perhaps a friend or relative. Use the questions, not as criticism, but as friendly advice. Then apply the advice to yourself.

I am neither promoting a fitness program nor proposing any specific form of exercise. You may walk, run, swim, do calisthenics. You might participate in sports such as volley ball and tennis, or work out with weights or gymnastic equipment. The form of exercise isn't important as long as your body moves vigorously enough to increase your heart and breathing rate appreciably and long enough to work up a good sweat. In the past you may have thought you were "stealing" time for these activities; now you may schedule the time without anxiety and guilt.

If you have been working in a sedentary occupation for

a long time, move into your exercise program gradually. If you choose running, don't try for the four-minute mile. Walk first. Then increase your walking distance. And when that feels comfortable, walk for a while and run only part of the way.

Consult your doctor before embarking upon any new ambitious exercise program. For anyone past thirty five or forty years of age, it may be wise to begin by exercising every other day to give your body time to recuperate and rebuild muscle between workouts. Do not try to set endurance records or compare yourself with someone else's performance until you have accustomed your body to the new routine. If you do it gradually, you will gain the most satisfaction from your improvement. This will come in a number of ways:

- Exercise will restore tone to your muscles.
- Your body will take on a more pleasing shape as muscle replaces fat.
- Exercise will strengthen your heart, lungs, and blood circulation.
- Your energy will be recharged.

The most important benefit will be the good feeling of being young, fresh and supple.

Along with these rewards—if you follow a consistent exercise plan in the free time you've gained from your time management program—you will also experience an increase in self-esteem. You will like yourself better because you have found the will to make a positive change in your health.

## Nutrition

As with the previous quiz on physical exercise, answer the following questions:

1. Do you limit eating of products made with "enriched" white flour and refined sugar?
2. Do you try to avoid foods high in artificial coloring, preservatives, and other chemical agents?
3. Do you take vitamins and food supplements regularly?
4. Do you include roughage (raw vegetables and rough grain) in your diet?
5. Do you avoid junk foods and advise other members of your family not to eat them?
6. Do you include a wide variety of vegetables and fruits in your diet?
7. Do you try to reduce consumption of red meat?
8. Do you chew and savor your food instead of gulping it down?
9. Do you know your optimum daily consumption of calories, protein, fat, carbohydrates, vitamins, and minerals?

As before, this quiz is not meant to test your knowledge of nutrition but rather to raise your level of awareness. Doctors often seem to place a low emphasis on diet, particularly in the controversial areas of meat, fats, and sugar. Ultimately, you are responsible for studying and following the best diet for *you*.

Most of us are so busy dealing with routine and everyday pressures that we do not take time to select foods that are good for us. However, thinking of yourself as the most important person in the world and planning ways to achieve a longer, healthier life can be one of the most valuable ways of using your hours of creative procrastination.

Losing weight may be one motivation for changing diet. It is a worthy motive but, unfortunately, many men and women fall prey to the multitude of fad diets promulgated by television, newspapers, and books. Many people have become discouraged because they tried various ones, yet none seemed effective over a long period. The drastic changes in eating styles may actually be more harmful than if no diet changes were attempted, and the discouragement from failure leads to lowered self-esteem. The objective is rather a permanent change in the kinds and quantities of food you eat, just as the objective in time management is to create a permanent improvement in your life.

The basic premise of health consciousness is that you take control of yourself. You are not dependent on pills to put you to sleep at night and arouse you in the morning. If you use your earned free time for daily exercise and developing a better diet, you will experience a synergistic effect. The combined result will be greater than the component parts: better health will propel you into greater productivity, which then frees even more time in which you can improve yourself.

## Relaxation

The following set of questions is designed to help you come to terms with stress, another vital component of whole body wellness. While there may be a fine line between tolerable stress (which improves productivity) and intolerable stress (which paralyzes), the borderline may be controlled through daily relaxation.

1. Can you identify five things that cause unpleasant stress in your personal or professional life?
2. Can you identify five recurring situations or conditions that cause you anxiety or frustration?
3. Can you visualize ways to change your daily life, or relationships with others, in order to ease or eliminate any of this stress, anxiety, or frustration?
4. Do you know that insomnia, fatigue, back pain, muscle stiffness, headaches, ulcers, colitis, gastritis, heart

disease, cancer, and strokes are often associated with stress?

5. Are you free most of the time from tension, frustration, aimlessness, and dissatisfaction with your work?

6. Did you take at least two weeks of vacation during the past year?

7. Were you able to relax and enjoy your vacation, or did you feel uneasy until you returned to work?

8. Do you feel that you deserve to relax and take time for yourself? (Creative procrastination.)

9. Do you meditate or sit quietly to clear your mind of work and problems at least once each day?

10. Have you experienced a massage for relaxation within the past six months?

11. Do you have nervous tics or mannerisms that are associated with tension and stress?

12. Do you sleep soundly, seldom feel tired, enjoy a good appetite, and deal satisfactorily with pressure?

It is a peculiar commentary on our culture, as we move toward a shorter work week and increased leisure time, that most people do not know (or have forgotten) how to relax and enjoy free time for its actual function—renewal and recuperation. The attitude of the American worker is that he can justify rest or play in terms of returning to do a better job. The European, by contrast, seems to enjoy vacation as a pleasure in its own right. He may be more likely to work for the express purpose of being able to afford to play in a more affluent style.

The American attitude is especially visible in the workaholic, who is anxious and uncomfortable when out of a work environment. The exaggerated conscience and scruples of this person will not permit relaxation. He may go through the motions of a vacation beside a mountain lake without actually relaxing or relishing it. The same muscular tension or headache he had when he left, will be with him when he comes home. This is also true of the *negative* procrastinator, who steals time and wastes it because of guilt about undone work. That is why it is so important to manage your routine so free time is really free. Then train yourself in relaxation methods you can use every day.

There are many popular books dealing with relaxation and meditation techniques. Some methods are borrowed from mystic Eastern cultures which are appealing because they seem so different from the pill-popping culture of the West. One technique is transcendental meditation, which requires training and using a private word or mantra. Another is yoga, which involves intricate muscle stretching and meditation. A third method is self-hypnosis. A fourth, which combines Western technology and Eastern mysticism, is biofeedback. This is not primarily a relaxation system, but it does enable the practitioner to monitor his or her own brain waves and rhythm while trying to change an involuntary function of the body.

Some meditation systems may be faddish, but most are useful to some degree. Choose a technique that helps you to relax and enjoy while doing it. You don't need to take an expensive course of instruction to accomplish this. With guidance, you can learn the best relaxation method for you. In my approach as a counselor I combine five methods of relaxation: proper breathing, rhythm, progressive relaxation, principles of self-hypnosis, and guided imagery.

In my sessions, I recommend seven to ten minutes of deep relaxation twice a day—another beneficial use for creative procrastination. First, I guide patients through the sequence, advising them to record tapes of their own voice guiding themselves into relaxation. The values of this are two-fold: the person uses familiar words to which he can respond naturally, and he gives instructions to himself. He *takes control* rather than taking directions from someone else. You can relax effectively by carrying out the following exercise step by step.

Sit in your most comfortable chair, or couch, or on the floor. Then just let go. Yawn, if you need to yawn, and stretch. Stretch and yawn and then check to feel any tight muscle knots in your body. Massage your back and shoulder muscles a little, and rub your knots, especially in the neck and back.

Stretch again, close your eyes and sit in the position most comfortable for you. Make sure your feet are straight and resting firmly on the floor. Put your arms in a slumped position and just sink into the chair, closing your eyes.

Start breathing. Inhale deeply then exhale, very slowly, and count: inhale (one, two, three, four) exhale (one, two three, four). Inhale slowly and exhale. As you do this, feel that air is spreading through your body, entering each part —your legs and stomach, your hands and head. Be in rhythm. Inhale, exhale. And clear your mind.

Continue this slow, rhythmic breathing and as you do, think of a word to say to yourself. It may be any simple word that is easy, comfortable, and pleasant, such as peace, or love, or rest. Now incorporate this word with your breathing, saying it quietly to yourself each time you inhale. Continue with this to clear your mind. Think of nothing but your word. Focus on this word while you're breathing to unclutter your mind. Let your simple word replace any distracting thought that may try to intrude.

As you do that, begin the next step, progressive relaxation. First, firmly tighten the muscles in the lower part of your foot. Keep breathing slowly, evenly, and saying your word. Then release the foot muscles. Now tighten the upper part of your foot as much as you can, and let go. Tense your other foot, as tightly as you can, and let go. Follow by tightening the muscles of your legs, first one and then the other, and release them.

Continue doing the same thing to other parts of your body. Tighten your buttocks, your stomach muscles, your legs, arms, and hands, and at the same time breathe evenly and say your word.

Tighten one entire side of your body and release it. Then the other. Stretch one side of your body—leg and arm on the left side—and relax. Then stretch the right side and relax. Continue this at your own pace until you feel that all of your muscles have been progressively tightened and released.

Now close your eyes and squeeze your eyelids tightly shut (this is part of hypnosis induction). Tighten and tighten until your eyes are glued shut. When you want to open your eyes you cannot because they are glued shut.

Keep breathing evenly and saying your word, now you sink into the chair, heavier and heavier. Your eyes are closed tightly and you cannot open them. You are heavier and heavier and sink into a heavy lump feeling.

Now you are relaxed. You may indulge yourself and be free to take any pleasure you would like. You may go in your mind to a quiet place like the ocean, enjoying the warm sand and listening to the rhythmic boom of the surf. You may swim lightly on the waves. Or you may choose to sit on top of a high mountain and contemplate the beauty of the world around you. In this state of relaxation, you may go wherever you wish and do whatever you choose.

Stay with your breathing—slowly inhale and exhale. Say your chosen word and remain in a quiet place. Enjoy yourself and be very quiet. Your eyes are still tight shut and heavy. Your mind is very clear. There are no thoughts in your mind.

As a few minutes pass you come back to awareness of the room. Open your eyes slowly. Take your time because they are tightly closed. Stretch leisurely and come back.

If you practice this relaxation exercise for 10 minutes

twice each day you will soon find your body and mind responding to work and problem solving with greater ease. Learn your optimum degree of awareness and—as a result of periodic relaxation—you will become more active, productive, and punctual in your work.

## Life-Style

The final element in total health is changing your life-style so that you are in harmony with your body, your time, and your life goals. Answer the following questions to determine if your life-style is attuned, or opposed, to what you wish to achieve.

1. Are you generally satisfied with your work, your mate and family, and your sense of purpose?
2. Are there people in your life with whom you can openly discuss your problems, triumphs, and disappointments?
3. Do you look forward to leisure time, weekends, outings with children, as well as occasions to be alone?
4. Do you consider personal relationships, family closeness and self-improvement more important than money, power and success?
5. Can you laugh at yourself?
6. Do you take physical risks, such as participating in strenuous sports on the weekend, after you haven't exercised for a while?
7. Do you respect and observe the 55-miles-per-hour speed limit on the highway?
8. Do you drive when angry or depressed?
9. Do you keep loaded firearms in your home or car?
10. Do you smoke? Cigarettes? Pipe? Cigars?
11. Do you drink alcohol? How much and how often?
12. Do you use mood-altering drugs, such as marijuana

or pep pills, on a regular or habitual basis? Do you use them for recreation?

13. Do you suffer from insomnia and, if so, do you resort to sleeping pills? By doctor's prescription? Over-the-counter remedies?

14. Do you take aspirin when you have a headache?

15. Do you ever question the need for prescribed medications?

16. Do you take care of your teeth and see a dentist for regular checkups?

17. Do you have a physical exam periodically?

18. Do you believe people can *choose* to live well or that they are controlled by destiny and environment?

19. Can you say "no" to other people without feeling guilty?

20. Do you often say "yes" to requests for volunteer service even when you know it will be difficult to follow through?

21. Do you believe that your attitude, along with the natural resistance of your body and mind, is as important in healing as are the medical arts?

22. Do you feel you are a winner with respect to life in general? Why do you feel this way?

23. Do you agree that most good things require effort, self-discipline, time, perseverence and sometimes foregoing other options?

24. Do you believe that your behavior can alter the usual pattern of degeneration due to aging?

25. If you could obtain health insurance that provided less compensation for sickness, but paid for wellness initiatives, would you buy it?

26. Are you concerned about world problems such as population growth and birth control?

27. Would you readily agree to major surgery if your doctor recommended it, or would you feel comfort-

able asking for a second, or even a third, opinion?

28. Do you believe that more doctors, better hospitals, and sophisticated equipment automatically guarantee better medical care?

29. If you knew you were terminally ill, would you prefer to die naturally with pain management, or would you wish to be kept "alive" as long as possible with drugs, machines, or other instrumentation?

These self-assessment questions were framed to help you examine your actions and attitudes about the whole framework of your life. You may find that your way of living is healthy and that you are already doing things that will lead you steadily toward your long-term goals. However, the questions may instead have revealed holes or lapses in your living pattern. Don't ignore or rationalize away these discrepancies. It isn't enough, for example, to be an efficient time organizer if your nutrition is poor, you don't get regular exercise, or you fail to manage the physical and mental aspects of stress.

If you have an addictive habit, such as smoking or consumption of alcohol and other drugs, there is a big fault in your overall health.

A wellness life-style requires thought about how well we sleep and how much sleep we need. Actually, the point is not how many hours of sleep, but how sound and free of worry that sleep is. Researchers have shown that most people probably sleep longer than they should for best health. If we follow our own natural rhythm for going to bed and arising, we may find even more hours for creative procrastination. Many people who claim to suffer insomnia actually do not, they simply fail to follow their body's natural rhythms.

Also included in your life-style are personal relations with a spouse, children, work associates, and friends, and the giving, caring, listening attitude with which you respond to each.

You are responsible for designing your life-style so that you can accomplish everything you need to do, while including free time for yourself.

# 3

# Dilemmas of Time Management

Our daily race with the clock is a major stress-inducing element. Stress, in turn, has been blamed for the distress which can lead to both physical and psychological illness. There never seems enough time to do what must be done, let alone finding some quiet time to be by ourselves or with others, to enjoy leisure and personal relationships.

Shirley, for example, is a middle-management executive who feels that she must perform nonstop at top efficiency. She arrives at work half an hour early every morning, partially to impress her supervisor but also to catch up with work left over from yesterday. She whirls through the day without taking a break for lunch.

By mid-afternoon, Shirley has a headache and stiff back. She becomes curt and short-tempered and her associates do not like to be near her. When they go home at five, she remains at her desk for an hour overtime.

Now she is caught in a dilemma: she feels guilty because she hasn't completed her work and guilty for coming home late to her family. As a forced compromise, Shirley fills her briefcase with work, hoping for a few quiet hours at home to finish. However, she finds her husband angry and the children cranky because dinner isn't ready. Dinner is nervous and tense, a task to be hurried through just as Shirley has hurried through the rest of her day. Later she can't sleep because she worries about tomorrow.

Such patterns, with minor variations, are the habits of hard-working men and women who live by the principle that industriousness is next to godliness. However, constant busy motion does not insure effective use of your time. Often the faster you run, the less efficient you become.

## The Tightening Spiral

A person caught up in the work ethic may eventually become incapable of finding time to think or relax alone. The result is an ever-tightening spiral of work, less leisure time, pressure, frustration, mistakes, guilt, anxiety, and illness. The spiral grows tighter with lost time, more pressure, more anxiety, more guilt, serious illness, and possibly death.

In fighting the clock and the calendar, we are like a watch spring which, when wound too tightly, finally breaks. The break may mean the "death" of a good job. It may mean death of a marriage. Or it may mean death, period.

Some people do work themselves to death. The high incidence of gastric ulcers and heart failure among business executives is not an accident of statistics. The cause and effect relationship is real. There are times when you must stop running in order to evaluate and come to terms with the need for leisure, for creative procrastination. This may be the most creative time of your life.

The higher you move on the executive or professional ladder, the more important it becomes to make time your servant rather than your master.

## Myths and Truths

Many men and women drift through their lives with a faulty road map, or without even being aware that there are ways to map the uses of time. We are frequently misguided by myths: since there is so little time we must use all of it; the harder we work, the more we will get done; and it is a sin to sit, think, and plan. Operating under such myths, a manager may turn down a golf date with a prospective client because he feels the office cannot operate without his presence. An engineer may concentrate fruitlessly on solving a design problem when an hour's walk in the woods might clear his head and suggest a better approach.

No matter how intelligent or capable a person may be, habits of behavior form around the myths of time and may then become locked in. In order to make better use of time, it is necessary to break misguided habits. There are some valid concepts regarding time.

- Time is one of our most precious resources and it should be used to our greatest personal, individual advantage.
- You must master yourself before you can master time. This means disciplining yourself toward achieving your objectives.
- Greater control of time provides greater freedom.
- Judge work by *results* instead of the time spent doing it.
- Incessant activity is not necessarily the same thing as effectiveness. The insecure person may compensate

for ineffectiveness by frantic activity that gives the illusion of accomplishment.

- Ten minutes spent in planning may save an hour of work.
- Because time is free, we often underestimate its value.
- A task or assignment tends to expand or condense according to the amount of time available.
- A person gravitates toward enjoyable things and away from unpleasant duties.
- There is always enough time to achieve the most important thing in life and for thinking, planning and relaxation.
- Life's greatest satisfaction comes through the balanced use of time.

## Scheduling Time

Most high achievers ignore the need to take time for themselves. However, as stated earlier, I believe that taking time for oneself can be positive and creative when it is planned and practiced with a higher level motive in mind than those which normally drive us at work.

For instance, a research scientist who sits with his feet propped up on his desk might be considered a procrastinator. But the ideas which result from apparent indolence may be of the highest value, both to him and his organization. Our most creative moments often occur when we give ourselves permission to procrastinate positively *without feeling guilty*. Earlier we saw Shirley as she fought a losing battle with the clock. Now let's look at another person who has learned to use discretionary time in a positive, creative, regenerative way.

Judy goes to bed at a reasonable hour, awakens to a clock radio in the morning, and leaves time for coffee, a leisurely breakfast, and reading the paper. She also allots sufficient time to drive to work so that she will start her day relaxed.

At the office she chats briefly with her associates and outlines the morning's work priority. For a break she takes a walk instead of drinking coffee. At noon, instead of waiting in line at a restaurant, she eats a sack lunch and reads under a tree. She may use half an hour for exercise or personal errands.

After lunch Judy again compares the day's planned work schedule against actual achievement. If a meeting lasted longer than it should have, she analyzes ways to shorten future meetings. At the end of the day she allows 10 minutes to plan tomorrow's work and then stops at 5 P.M. She does not carry work home; the evening is for husband and family.

Judy knows, however, that she first needs a short time to unwind, so she plays a set of tennis, swims for thirty minutes, or works out at an exercise salon. Her husband anticipates this as part of her daily routine and knows that when his wife comes home she will be re-energized and ready to give herself fully to him and the family. By controlling their time during the day, they can give more to each other—and ask more—without tension or stress.

## Positive Pressure

Pressure and stress resulting from ineffective use of time can lead to mental and physical debility. However, with the concept of creative procrastination comes an awareness that pressure and stress can also be positive if approached from the proper viewpoint and attitude.

We know that periods of pressure and tension inevitably will occur in our lives. Therefore, it is up to us to learn how to cope with pressure as a positive force. If we were not subjected to some pressure, either self-imposed or imposed by others, few of us would accomplish anything. Everyone works best under a certain level of pressure. It is our duty to define that level and to know in advance the amount of stress we can tolerate without becoming frustrated, fearful, and ineffective.

Through experience and experimentation you can determine the pressure plateau at which you work best and most comfortably, and to recognize danger signals when the stress level is too high. Stress can result, for example, from a project which must be completed before a certain deadline. Some people, dreading the task, put it off (negative procrastination) until there is absolutely not enough time left to do the work. One way to circumvent this tendency is to set artificial deadlines. If we set them earlier than the assigned time—and perform according to our schedule—the work will be well-prepared by the time it is due. We reap the reward of satisfaction in performing well and knowing that we controlled time rather than letting it control us.

Susan, a thirty-year-old mother of two children, is a good example of how pressure can work to advantage. She is taking part-time classes to complete her university education, and must write a long term paper. She hates writing papers and fears that her effort will not please her instructor or meet her own high standards. She postpones starting the assignment, she feels guilty, and her anxiety mounts.

Finally the approaching deadline presses Susan to make two decisions. First, she will now marshal her creative forces and work steadily to complete the paper because if she doesn't, her punishment will be failing the course. Her second decision is to accept herself as a fallible human being and realize that even if her paper does not get an A, she will still be okay. Pressure situations often help people accept their limitations and realize their strengths, focus attention, and teach realistic time apportioning.

Susan suffered severe headaches while postponing her job, but once she determined to get at it, the headaches disappeared. She also discovered that working under more time pressure (but less pressure for excellence) actually helped her produce a better paper than she had anticipated.

## Reward and Punishment

A change from negative stress to positive stress can only be brought about through a change in attitude. If you adopt a positive approach and anticipate pressure situations, they can actually help focus thought and energy on a problem. The more you can use *artificial deadlines* as tools to solve a problem, the more you can use pressure to your advantage.

Establish your own system of reward and punishment. In Susan's case, her reward was the satisfaction of completing a task she disliked. Her punishment would have been failing the class. When working with artificial deadlines, set up actual rewards and denials such as: "If I don't finish this assignment on time, I'll deny myself golf for a week," or "When this job is done, I'll go out and buy a new dress (or suit) because I'll deserve it." Write down the punishment and rewards you assign yourself and keep both sides of the equation in proportion to the importance of the task. This is part of the process of taking control and assuming responsibility for how you use time rather than simply reacting to demands from your environment.

A person producing a marketing research report for the next meeting of the board of directors, may do one of two things: First, worry about it until emotionally paralyzed, saying, "I'll never be able to do it anyway, so what's the point of trying?" Or say: "I know that I work best under pressure. The board meeting is two weeks from now, so a week before that I'll stop everything else, tell other people not to interrupt me, and work eight hours a day on this project."

## Allowing Rational Lead Time

Creating positive pressure requires still one more ingredient—giving yourself adequate lead time. Some people squeeze themselves too tightly under pressure, perhaps allowing only a day to finish a project that would realistically require two or three days. The ability to set rational deadlines involves several factors:

- Learning your capabilities and how much you can accomplish in a given time.
- Determining how much stress you can handle, and when you need to assert yourself to decline a task.
- Taking advantage of what you learn each time you complete a difficult job satisfactorily.

## The Depression Syndrome

The opposite of taking control of your time and life is losing control entirely.

Sometimes the short-term rush of events and problems does become uncontrollable, but if this happens consistently over a long period of time, we are apt to sink into depression. We feel paralyzed, drowning under an intolerable overload. You really may be overloaded with work, or even in the wrong job, but when you lose control of time, everything becomes overwhelming.

The person who gets up in the morning wondering anxiously what will "happen" today is typical. This person has no schedule or plan, only a vague feeling of aimlessness. There is nothing exciting to look forward to, and the temptation is to stay in bed, recounting all the miserable things in life and anticipating more of the same. Without a stimulating promise in the future, we tend to slip into apathy and depression.

When depressed, you become hypersensitive to all demands, including small duties such as changing a car tire or driving to work. An unexpected problem can appear unsurmountable. You cry inwardly, "Leave me alone! I don't need one more thing to do."

This accomplishes nothing, of course, except to accelerate depression.

The opposite kind of person wakes up in the morning and says: "I'll look at this day before it happens. If I feel like working, I'll work. If I feel like playing, I'll play. I might just take two hours for myself. I'm not anxious about what will happen because I know I can control my day, take time for myself, and still do what must be done."

The way to draw yourself out of depression is to be *realistic*. How much can you really do every day? Once you have established that reality, you should stop piling up work you know you can't do. How much can you do while achieving that precious balance of free time for yourself? Most people can work only ninety concentrated minutes at a time at optimum performance. Knowing that, it becomes natural (and you don't have to feel guilty about it) to take a few minutes for coffee, reading, or contemplating the beautiful day. This is a part of your natural rhythm which must be respected if you are to do your best.

A professional woman, for instance, may suffer depression because her house is not clean according to her standards, or her flower garden is dying from neglect. She had tried, unsuccessfully, to do everything at once.

The solution may be to have a smaller garden, or learn to look a weed in the face without guilt. She may even have to give up gardening because she has too many other high priority items to absorb her energy and time. She must decide what is important and follow a set of priorities. Something has to give in favor of something else. Instead of staring impotently at uncompleted projects, she must make a commitment to her own life.

This is a decision you must make every day. Part of avoiding depression is learning to *assert yourself* because if you are a "nice" person, victimized by circumstances and other people's demands, they will demand forever. At work a person must say: "I'm sorry, but I can't take on another assignment today. I've got everything I can handle. Perhaps we can discuss it tomorrow." You may be fearful to make such a statement to your superior but it's essential if you are to work at your optimum level. Chances are your boss will respect you for it if you have a record of good performance.

A husband may say to his wife: "I'm sorry, but I can't run those errands for you because my day is loaded. Perhaps we can do them together during the weekend."

Or a mother to her family: "I'm not going to do anymore for all of you today because this is my free time, and I'm going to play bridge." That's okay. Everyone in her family will survive. She's going to socialize for a few hours because she knows this helps her to relax, to take care of herself, and she doesn't feel guilty. She will return to her family refreshed and even more giving. Again, it's a commitment to life.

## Changing Negative Stress

A person under negative stress is in a defensive position, asking: How will they see me? How will they judge me? How will they evaluate me? These questions are asked fearfully, without questioning whether "they" are qualified to judge. The person is anxious, visualizing catastrophic results and failing to see events and circumstances in a clear perspective. Under negative stress, an executive may hesitate to try innovative techniques because he fears the boss's reaction.

In fearing that his work will not be satisfactory, he will create a self-fulfilling prophecy. The person under negative stress is always on edge and at the verge of breakdown, tending very often to develop irrational and superstitious fears.

All of this relates to time management because the person who lives continually under the whip of negative stress is, in a sense, paralyzed; he or she is so afraid of life that small commitments appear as large as a mountain. Tasks seem unreasonably difficult, and the person feels incompetent. Managing time is impossible because it appears to be just one more insurmountable task.

The answer to this is to first begin managing small portions of time, gradually increasing the scope of control. If you are faced by a mountain, try controlling first a pebble, then another, and so on until you feel competent to tackle all of it.

Ron, for example, sought counseling about a work problem.

"I'm always anxious," he said. "There are so many demands that I don't know how to get out from under them. I'm sinking. I'm missing deadlines and I'm going to be fired."

He was advised to take a small portion of each day and try to organize that so he could work effectively. He started with the period from 8 to 11 A.M. As he studied that three-hour period, he learned to eliminate long phone conversations and extended meetings. He organized his desk neatly and refused to confront more work clutter than he could accommodate at one time. He screened incoming mail and consigned seventy five percent of it to the waste basket instead of filing it for future consideration. His morning changed so successfully that he extended his time planning through the remainder of the day. Lunch time and coffee breaks turned into enjoyable free time which he could use without anxiety, worry, or guilt. Instead of feeling guilty for wasting time, we need to accept the belief that the better the balance achieved between leisure and work, the more productive and successful one will be.

## The Efficient Robot

Another product of relinquishing control of time is the efficient robot. This person does everything compulsively, in patterns built upon habitual response to demands upon time. On the surface his time management seems superb. He keeps a log accounting for every minute. He compulsively checks his log and appointment book to make sure he doesn't waste a second. And he becomes so good at it that he leaves no time for human interaction or relaxation.

The efficient robot forgets the human side of time management. He never listens to his body rhythms, his tired back, or the tight muscles which remind him to get up and stretch for five minutes.

Such people may be excellent at only a narrow range of work. They may be top executives who are in too much of a hurry to talk calmly with other people or pay attention to their spouses and children. Often their marriages and family life break down. They are successful, bright, and have all the right degrees, but they do not allow for the balance of leisure and good feeling. They run efficiently, but not effectively.

There may seem to be a fine line between the efficient robot, who is a slave to structured time, and another person who also organizes time but sets aside moments or hours for him or herself. But the difference is exactly that. The creative procrastinator works his schedule so that there is time not only for work, but also for listening to natural rhythms, and for successful relationships with other people.

We mentioned how the tyranny of time squeezes you into

a paralyzed corner of ever-smaller achievement. Now we can consider its opposite. As you become more confident in controlling time, the more you protect it, the more of it you have, the more you're respected, the more you accomplish, and the more you can be generous in the end toward other people—because you have *taken care of your needs first.*

Say yes to yourself and no to others. Be assertive. Take time for yourself according to plan; not because of fear or negative pressures.

# 4

# Productivity and Planning

"How much of what quality work must I produce in a given period of time?"

This question defines the limits of any problem that involves planning and productivity, whether you are the president of an electronics company, middle-management engineer, small-business person, doctor, or lawyer.

Now add another small twist to the question: "How little time can I work to satisfy external demands, leaving the remainder of each day for creative pursuits?"

These questions begin to diverge from standard rules postulating that success comes only through endless, concentrated work. The divergence is intentional because many people plunge into work mechanically without considering the relative importance of each task or sensing how much time should be devoted to it. This tendency is not limited to the lower echelons of an organization. Many managers and professional people also tackle work haphazardly, reaching for the top piece of paper in the in-basket, and then working through the pile without pausing to reflect on which task or project promises the most important end result.

When such a person reaches a task that is distasteful, difficult or boring, the tendency is to shuffle it back to the bottom of the pile—with a promise to give it more attention later. This woman or man may wander around the office or read nonessential mail while feeling anxious and guilty for not dealing with the main problem.

In much of the business world, we seem to emphasize quantity rather than quality of work. We also seem obsessed with processes rather than end results. There is a lack of creative awareness that problems might be solved in a few minutes rather than consuming hours or days.

As stated by Sebastian de Grazia, psychologist with The Twentieth Century Fund: "The clock's presence everywhere, and its tie to the factory with its relatively unskilled work, soon gave rise to the idea that one was selling time as well as, or rather than, skill. The lightening of toil and simplifying of tastes brought about by machines gave a related impression: that one was selling time rather than labor. The hourly rate and the piece rate also express these notions. So time begins to be money and, like money, a valuable, tangible, commodity to be saved, spent, earned and counted. . . . No other nation by now is as precise in its time sense nor so time conscious as the United States."*

## Working to Objective

As de Grazia suggests, machines, computers, and other "time savers" have obscured the fact that it is human skill and innovative ability that we are buying and selling. To

---

*Sebastian de Grazia, *Of Time, Work and Leisure* (New York: Doubleday, 1962), pp. 305–311.

what end are we earning, spending, and saving time? If productivity is the desired result, it should start from the following point of view: *It's not how much time you spend working, but how well planned, organized, and motivated you are to produce what is expected, or what you expect of yourself.*

"Many businessmen and managers," states Ross Webber, "are especially driven by their need for achievement, by desiring to apply their time to challenging problems, to offer novel solutions and to obtain gratifying feedback on what they have accomplished within a reasonable time. . . . They still have the problem of judging when this activity-filled time is being used rightly or wrongly."*

## Emotional Blocks

Negative procrastination involves mental or emotional blocks which prevent you from working effectively. These blockages are self-defeating, you inflict mental torture upon yourself.

For example, John is administrative assistant to the president of an electronics company. He has been requested to write a work-flow plan for assembling a new line of components. He believes his future growth with the company depends upon how well he develops this plan.

John suffers stage fright and concern that his end product will not be good enough to please the president. He is afraid of being less than perfect and exposing himself to criticism. John is uncertain how to begin, and embarrassed to ask more experienced men for advice and guidance.

When he received the assignment, John's deadline was a month away, but each time he approached the subject it seemed overwhelming. He put it off, turning to other rou-

---

*Ross A. Webber, *Time and Management* (New York: Van Nostrand Reinhold, 1972), p. 19.

tine work, and rationalizing that one day he would be "inspired" to proceed with the work-flow plan.

John's time slipped away until only three days remained. Then he began writing in desperation, throwing together disjointed ideas to get "something" on paper. He swamped his secretary with typing as he tore up and revised successive drafts of the plan. In the end he pleased neither himself nor the company president.

In contrast, Frank examined a similar assignment and checked the calendar to see how much time he had to complete the job. He noted separate elements—including research and interviews with associates—which needed to be accomplished before he could write the final report. Then he assigned a day to complete each of the elements in order.

Frank took into account his own personal work rhythm, recognizing that he could concentrate only for an hour or two at a time. He planned breaks ranging from 15 minutes to an hour during which he would turn to other more enjoyable work or simply relax. He scheduled the work in segments and as he proceeded he gained confidence that the total job would be done on time. He accepted the possibility that the final result might not be perfect, but it would serve its purpose. He finished ahead of deadline and was congratulated for performing well.

The difference between the two is that Frank did not permit himself to become overwhelmed by the complexity of the task. He retained control by taking the job in successive steps and rewarding himself with earned blocks of free time to regenerate his interest. John did not know how to begin and became emotionally paralyzed each time he tried.

It sometimes requires only a small push or spark of motivation to overcome the fear of starting. If you are among the millions who procrastinate negatively because you don't

know how to begin, here is a list of ways to help
project:

1. Schedule specific time on your calendar for the job.
2. Think through the problem: define it, and explain it
   in a memo to yourself.
3. Establish priorities; keep the overall objective in
   mind.
4. Locate the most important item and start there.
5. Ask an associate for suggestions; ask your supervisor
   for ideas and suggestions; discuss the problem with
   your secretary who may well have a fresh viewpoint.
6. Arrange a meeting to clarify what needs to be done.
7. Categorize files and information pertinent to the job.
8. Try letting your mind wander idly around the problem without pressure for instant achievement; use
   your normal "worrying" time to work on the project.
9. Identify what prevents you from starting.
10. Make a clear decision each day on what you are will-
    ing to do *now* on the project.
11. List sub-tasks; start with the simplest one and do it
    now.
12. Reward yourself for getting started.
13. Give your first minutes every morning to the project,
    or that time of day when you are usually at your best.
14. Confer with a consultant in time management.
15. Hire someone to help.
16. Assign part of the project to a subordinate.
17. Write a status report on the work.
18. Consider how you may benefit from successful com-
    pletion of the project.
19. Do the most important part of the project, even if it
    is distasteful, and *do it now*.

Often a small positive action is all that is necessary to

break the log jam of mental blocks which thwart progress on a major task. Generally life is not made up of large projects but of a steady stream of large and small jobs. If you start and finish each one promptly, you will build self-confidence while creating more time for yourself.

An author friend remarked that he could find any number of excuses *not* to put the first sentence on a blank piece of paper. He would sharpen pencils, go to the bathroom, stare out the window, rearrange papers, or empty a waste basket rather than begin working. He might waste two hours of prime morning time fiddling around with trivial chores.

To break this habit, he resolved to write a first sentence immediately after entering his study—even if the sentence was nonsense. From this he moved on easily to the next one, knowing he could go back and edit what he had written. Because his work entailed a mental struggle, this author also established a set of penalties and rewards. He would not allow himself a time break or cup of coffee until he had finished one or more pages of manuscript. After this pre-planned production, he felt he had earned a break for creative procrastination.

He drew several benefits from the self-discipline. First, as he looked forward to a break, his production improved. Whereas he might have written no more than a paragraph in an hour, he now produced a page. As productivity improved, so did his self-esteem and confidence. The earned free time (which might be ten minutes or an hour) opened his mind to new ideas. It also provided time for reading and absorbing new information.

Principles for promptly starting and completing a task can apply in any occupation. A person may either lead a non-productive life, finding excuses for idleness, or by attacking the most important task first and progressing through the priority list, he can create time to do the projects most wanted and needed.

## Setting Goals

Any discussion of productivity must consider motivation, recognizing the signs and reasons for its absence.

Motivation is the drive to succeed, to progress towards a good end result. You may be motivated to make money, to build a house, to buy an expensive automobile, or to save money for your children's education. But more essentially, you are motivated to work because you want to feel good about what you are doing. An engineer, for example, may be partially motivated by the desire for a bigger pay check, but a stronger motivation originates from the urge to design a more elegant piece of machinery or electronic component. A good auto mechanic finds satisfaction in making a machine run well.

The way to sustain motivation is to work toward specific goals and objectives: are you interested and excited as you work toward your objectives; are the objectives yours personally, or imposed by others?

In work situations, goals usually are externally imposed—by your boss, your corporation, your need to earn a living. The ideal situation occurs when we are able to integrate personal needs and desires with external objectives so that they become essentially the same. We become interested in the assignment as it coincides with our own interests and wishes. Certainly, a product must be made or a project completed within a limited time; that's what work is. However, if we also have a personal interest in it, the process itself can be satisfying.


## Life Goals

To approach that happy situation, it is necessary to define what you want and need out of life. Take a moment to give yourself the following quiz:

1. Do I have a clearly defined set of lifetime goals? If not, write them down now. The question is important enough that you should take time to think it through. If this is a first attempt, the list may be fuzzy and incomplete but you can refine it later.

2. Do I have a congruent set of goals for the next six months? If not, think about them and write them down.

3. Have I done something today to move me closer to my lifetime goals? My short-term goals?

4. If not, why not?

5. Do I have a clear idea of what I want to accomplish during the coming week?

6. Do I concentrate on objectives instead of procedures, judge by achievement rather than by the amount of activity?

7. Do I try to do the most important tasks during my prime time, when I am strongest and most alert?

8. Do I set priorities according to importance rather than urgency?

9. How can I improve my performance?

10. How can I work more effectively toward my personal goals and objectives?

The last two questions are special. They will occur again as we go along, but they are placed here to help you discover that there is almost always more than one way to improve your work methods. One businessman, after taking this quiz, analyzed his work habits and realized that he had allowed long, unstructured staff meetings to crowd out more important work. He imposed a rule that meetings would begin and end at precise times and would conform (except in emergencies) to a pre-arranged agenda. He soon found he had time to spare for creative procrastination.

## The Time Log

You can't make decisions about improving performance until you study how you've been using your time. For this you need to keep a time log in some form such as that on the following pages.

You will need a number of these forms so it is best to lay out your own. They need not be elaborate so long as they leave room to note *all* of your activities during waking hours. If your normal routine is going to bed and rising earlier or later than is shown on the form, write the time log hours to conform to your habits. You may wish to change these habits later, but the present purpose of the log is to help you analyze how you are actually using time in contrast to how you would prefer to use it.

### DAILY RECORD OF USE OF TIME

Date _____

| | |
|---|---|
| 7:00–7:30 | |
| 7:30–7:45 | |
| 7:45–8:00 | |
| 8:00–8:15 | |
| 8:15–8:30 | |
| 8:30–8:45 | |
| 8:45–9:00 | |
| 9:00–9:15 | |
| 9:15–9:30 | |
| 9:30–9:45 | |
| 9:45–10:00 | |

| 10:00–10:15 | |
|---|---|
| 10:15–10:30 | |
| 10:30–10:45 | |
| 10:45–11:00 | |
| 11:00–11:15 | |
| 11:15–11:30 | |
| 11:30–11:45 | |
| 11:45–12:00 | |
| 12:00–12:15 | |
| 12:15–12:30 | |
| 12:30–12:45 | |
| 12:45–1:00 | |
| 1:00–1:15 | |
| 1:15–1:30 | |
| 1:30–1:45 | |
| 1:45–2:00 | |
| 2:00–2:15 | |
| 2:15–2:30 | |
| 2:30–2:45 | |
| 2:45–3:00 | |
| 3:00–3:15 | |
| 3:15–3:30 | |
| 3:30–3:45 | |

| 3:45–4:00 | |
| 4:00–4:15 | |
| 4:15–4:30 | |
| 4:30–4:45 | |
| 4:45–5:00 | |

*Evening:*

_____

*Notes:*

_____

_____

You may believe you have been using time wisely and efficiently, but you may also be surprised to see, in graphic form, how much of each day is lost in aimless or trivial activities. This exercise is divided into three parts: a log of *last* week, a day-by-day record of *this* week, and a schedule of how you expect (or would like) to use *next* week.

These time logs may seem overly time-consuming at first, but they will be worth the effort. They begin the adjustment towards a more productive future. As you remember last week, fill in every space for each day, whether or not you now think the time was well-spent. If you procrastinated negatively, be honest with yourself and write it down. Be *specific* about how you used the time. Your memory may not be reliable in some places, but do the best you can. If you can't remember how a certain hour was spent, that may indicate the hour contributed little of importance either in terms of work or in personal satisfaction. One thing the log will reveal is how much time you spend on habitual activities.

The second task is to begin keeping a record *today* of activities this week. Once you have completed the new week, compare the current time log with the old one to see if there were changes. Chances are, as you become more conscious of each hour, you will automatically begin improving your use of time.

The last third of the exercise is to fill out a time sheet according to how you expect or wish to use the week ahead. Again, be as explicit as possible. If you would like to change the number of hours you sleep, for example, make a note of when you intend to go to bed at night and rise in the morning.

In comparison with the logs from the past two weeks, do you now find that you are approaching a better balance between work and pre-planned time for creative procrastination? There will be few instant miracles, but this time log exercise is a start toward letting the past be your guide to the future. Feel free to continue the log for as many weeks or months as you feel necessary to help guide your time use. Make frequent comparisons between your *plan* and your actual performance. In this way you can begin realistically scheduling your hours, days, and weeks while keeping in mind both your personal goals and work objectives which may either be internally or externally generated.

## Making Your Time Log Work for You

Now begin making your time log work for you by asking yourself the following questions and writing down the answers:

1. *Is there any pattern in how I have been doing things?* Your

answer will be "yes," because whatever we do almost always results from an activity pattern. Certain habitual action, or inaction, prevents us from fulfilling our needs, and blocks us from using time for creative procrastination. Study your patterns and make notes that help you identify the patterns clearly. Be honest; you are the only person who needs to see the results.

2. *Am I willing to change hourly patterns that limit my productivity?* You *can* make this decision, and it is important. Are you ready for the pain and discomfort of admitting that "between 8 and 10 in the morning I typically waste time by aimlessly wandering and drifting about?" If you are willing to alter such a pattern, then you can safely believe your life will become different after several weeks. But you must make the commitment. Write it down and *sign* it.

3. *What are my problem areas?* This is where your time log can help diagnose where, when, and why things have been going wrong in your day. The problem areas, once you confront them, will also illuminate parcels of free time that you can use without guilt or anxiety.

4. *How can I do it differently?* First, why do you *want* to do it differently? Do you want more time to spend with friends? More time to relax on your job? More time to play golf? Do you want to be recognized and promoted? Or perhaps you simply wish to be more innovative in problem solving.

Whatever your motivation for change, the next step is to plan, setting down how much time is needed for each job so that you can complete it satisfactorily. For example, Jennifer says: "I like to paint for three or four hours every day. I also love to read and once a week I need to be with friends. While I have these high priorities, I also have to hold a job. Can I be more productive? Can I control my time so that I have the prime hours from 8 to 12 in the morning for painting and reading, then have lunch with a friend, and still do the rest of my work?" The fact is, she can.

Why can she do it while another person may fail? Because Jennifer uses her time log and plans each day's work and play. Then she works her plan. She exerts will power and is effective because she likes herself and feels she deserves time for herself. She wards off outside interruptions by being politely assertive, yet she is genuinely charming and caring for other people.

Much is possible if we control our use of time.

## Clarifying Expectations

Clarifying what we expect of ourselves, and what is expected of us by others, is part of building confidence in how we use time. We are often our severest critics. Our goals may be so high that we can never be pleased with what we do. Some people cannot accept compliments gracefully because they carry an internal blueprint which says: "I am not good enough." Here is an exercise to help measure your own expectations against achievement:

1. Are you pleased when you complete a piece of work?
2. Recall three major projects you have completed recently. List them and with each one answer the following:

   Which end results pleased me and which were failures?

   Which projects caused me to feel good about myself?

   What were my expectations in each case?
3. After completing a project, what type of adjective or phrase do you usually give yourself?

   Do you say: "It's okay," or "It's not bad"?

   Do you say: "I'm a failure," or "I'm unreliable"?

   Or do you say: "I'm excellent"?

Are you too strict with yourself, or too lenient? Are you being realistic? If your answer to question number one was "no," be a little easier with yourself. No one is perfect. In your answers to number three you may find your expectations were too high or too low. Chances are, if your work pleases your superiors, but not yourself, you are not being realistic.

Do you praise yourself enough? If you have done a really good job, you should be able to recognize it and give yourself credit. Some people are obsessed with the notion that their work is never adequate—a news release not telling enough, a sales presentation insufficiently hard-hitting, a financial analysis incomplete. But some people will add lines and color and figures until they destroy what was good.

But there is a certain point in any creative endeavor that, if passed, will detract from rather than enhance its beauty or utility.

During the next two weeks, try to be aware of the quality and excellence of everything you do. When you're done with each task, look at it, evaluate it and give yourself a score. You are free to give yourself an F or a C or an A+, but be honest about it. You may describe what you've done as "not bad," although we hope you will have gained enough confidence to give yourself a better grade than that.

The second set of expectations to which we must respond are those imposed from outside—by other people or the environment. We all need love and approval. Employees want to please their superiors. A husband and wife try to gratify each other. A child needs parental approbation. All of us seek our friends' admiration, and respect in our community.

Strive for a balance between internal and external expectations. Sometimes you will gain a greater reward by sticking to your own standards. In other situations, the return may be better if you adapt to external demands. The delicate balance between opposing expectations is most pertinent in the business world, especially in the ongoing employer-employee relationship. Suppose you have completed a project for your supervisor and, as you evaluate it, you say: "I think it's good. Perhaps not perfect, but as good as I can do. I suppose, though, that Joe will find something to criticize." Since the superior is generally critical, your hunch was right. Joe turned back the work with suggestions for improvement.

Now is the time to be in touch with the adult in you. Some men and women permit themselves to be victimized by extension of the child-parent relationship, but it is important not to respond as a child. If the supervisor's criticism is valid, use the occasion as a learning experience. On the other hand, if you are satisfied with the quality of your work, the boss may be wrong. Then you must say: "I hear your opinion and I appreciate it, but according to my standards, the work is good. It's the best I can do."

It is essential that you build confidence in your ability to plan and complete a project that fulfills your expectations. Someone else's comment may help you improve somewhat, but beyond that you have done your best and should not accept being put down continually. If you slip into that parent-child relationship, you worry about meeting your boss's expectations and have set yourself up for a lowered self-esteem and losing your creative free time. *His* expectations of *you* may also be built upon the parent-child extension, or merely his need to prove that he's the boss.

An illustration of that situation is a man who was a public relations executive for a large corporation. His superior, a vice-president, requested him to write a news release about the company's latest dividend announcement.

Because of governmental restrictions, the news release followed almost exactly the same three-paragraph form from one financial quarter to the next. The only changes needed involved current dates and figures.

The executive wrote the short release and submitted it. The vice-president sent it back for rewrite. After changing a few words and phrases, the writer submitted it again. The process of submittal and rejection continued for several hours. Finally, the 29th version of the news release was accepted, but it was identical to the first draft the writer had submitted.

The boss, because of his own insecurity, had to prove that he was boss. He managed by the doubtful direction of "show me something I like."

In the case of actual substandard work, however, remember you are human. It is part of being human to make mistakes, and part of living to learn from them. At the end of each day, ask yourself these questions:

- What things did I do today for which I deserve a pat on the back?
- Which activities today were poorly done?
- What should I learn from these situations in order to improve my performance?

## Coping with Criticism

Most of us associate mistakes with criticism because as children we were told: "You're a naughty child because you made a mistake." This is one of the milder forms of destructive criticism, implying that a person is evil because of a human error. It can lead to lack of confidence and contributes to the common problem of extending parent-child relationships into professional adult life.

If you receive such destructive criticism regularly you will spend time worrying about pleasing your supervisor instead of doing a job to the best of your ability. Too much time is wasted redoing tasks which should have been completed properly in the first place. If you apply destructive criticism to your employees, both your time and theirs is lost. Constructive criticism, in contrast, does not down the individual, but offers suggestions for improvement. The subordinate learns better techniques and gains confidence, becoming less fearful of, and dependent upon, his superior.

Because of destructive criticism received in the past, we tend to deny the possibility that we will make mistakes. We don't want to acknowledge them and, therefore, overlook ways to correct them and grow.

### Reviewing Time Use Habits

The exercises in this chapter have been aimed toward increasing your awareness of time use habits in connection with productivity and planning. To fix these thoughts more firmly, give yourself the following test. In addition to the "yes" and "no" answers, add columns on your paper for "sometimes" and "comments." You can't expect to undo unsatisfactory habits you have spent years developing in a few days or weeks. It will probably take at least six months before you notice that new time use habits have become a firm part of your life. Retaking the following test every six months will help measure your degree of change and prevent back-sliding into old patterns.

### Time Habit Quiz

1. Do I delegate as much work as possible?
2. Do I delegate challenging jobs as well as routine ones? Some executives are afraid to challenge subordinates with difficult work on the assumption that "they may be after my job." Remember, it's *your* time you're saving.
3. Do I delegate authority along with responsibility? Delegation of a task without giving your subordinate

the authority to follow through can cost you more time than if you did the job yourself.

4. Do I discourage employees from delegating *upward* decisions and tasks they find difficult?

5. Do I use subordinates effectively to gain better control of time?

6. Do I prevent unneeded information and publications from intruding on my time?

7. Do I follow the golden rule when filing material: When in doubt, throw it out?

8. In meetings do I define issues, simplify decisions, and assign specific responsibilities?

9. Do I try to settle business matters by phone or in person, writing letters and memos only when necessary?

10. Do I try to put work out of my mind when I'm away from the office?

11. Do I make minor decisions quickly?

12. Do I take steps to guard against recurring crises?

13. Do I set deadlines for myself and others?

14. Do I take time to plan?

15. Have I eliminated any unproductive routines or work processes lately? Many managers find it more comfortable to remain in accustomed ruts of procedure than to initiate new and more effective processes.

16. Do I keep work in my pocket or briefcase to which I can refer when I have moments to spare, such as waiting in line at a post office? (This practice is not the same as carrying an overload of work home from the office.)

17. Do I try to think of what needs to be done *now* instead of rehashing past errors or worrying about the future?

18. Do I use a time log to prevent slipping back into unproductive routines?

19. Do I try to establish new habits that will make me more effective?

20. Do I keep in mind the dollar value of my time? Vilfredo Pareto was an Italian nobleman and economist who lived from 1848 to 1923. He postulated that eighty percent of the world's important tasks were accomplished in twenty percent of the available time. My thesis modifies Pareto to suggest that sixty percent of the work can be done in thirty percent of the time, and the remaining work in sixty percent of the remaining available time. This leaves at least ten percent for your creative use or relaxation.

21. Do I apply the Pareto principle whenever I am confronted by a number of different projects?

22. Do I control my time, or are my actions dictated by other people's priorities?

23. Do I plan for, and deliberately *give* myself, some free time each day to use in any way I choose?

If you answered "no" to any of these twenty-three questions, review your time log and decide what you can do to correct the deficiency. The price of effective time management is continual vigilance. That's why you should retake this examination every six months. Think of it as you would a physical or dental checkup; the final result is fully as important.

# 5

# Managing Your Time Effectively

The basic check list for good time management includes:

- Awareness of time
- Thorough planning according to priorities
- Integration of time management with creative procrastination.

To manage your time effectively, it is important to remain conscious of how each hour is used. That also means maintaining a sharp awareness of your requirements within your personal and professional framework. Some managers and professionals have greater leeway than others in controlling their use of time. Therefore, precise awareness of your role in the scheme of your corporation or business is a prerequisite to gaining control of time, and adjusting it to satisfy your needs.

Without exception, however, every person will allow some time to escape without using it to advantage. Wasted time is like water dripping from a leaky faucet. A few lost drops don't seem serious, but when measured over a period of time the loss can be considerable and costly. Cost is measured according to the value you place upon your hours. If your work is worth $12 an hour, each wasted minute costs you 20 cents. So you may think of wasted time as time leaks in your life. It is time you failed to use because you did not establish or follow a clear schedule of priorities.

How many times have you said: "I could have finished the job today but . . .

- I just didn't have time.
- Joe came in and killed the morning.
- The boss called a meeting and there wasn't enough time left afterward.
- Reading the mail and dictating correspondence took so much time that I couldn't finish.

If you look at these typical excuses, you will see that in each case you gave away *control* and *responsibility*. You blamed an outside agency for wasting your time. Saying that something happened to you, or somebody did it to you, is placing yourself in the role of passive receptor. You're just there while events and people pass through *your* time.

You can correct this, first, by identifying your time leaks and, second, by stopping them so that you are no longer the passive victim but rather the controller.

### Your Place in Management Structure

Before beginning a detailed inspection of your time leaks, you must define where you fit in the managerial structure, and the extent to which you are able to control your behavior. Time use specialists have broken down management and supervision into six general types or styles:

1. General executives
2. Sales managers
3. Functional control managers—those with special expertise in such areas as engineering, finance, industrial relations, or accounting
4. Service managers—those in mid-level positions who provide service for primary operating departments
5. Operating supervisors—mid-level line managers
6. Staff specialists—professionals who are often involved in managerial decisions

At all levels of supervision, communications consume the greatest amount of time. Your discretion in using time depends greatly upon your skills in communicating with your superiors, associates, subordinates, and people outside the company.

## Levels of Communication

The general executive spends more time communicating with people than any other manager, especially responding to others with advice and discussion. The general manager often spends more time at work than other members of his staff.

Functional control managers and staff specialists are involved in the widest *variety* of communications. They are able to move outside the chain of command and learn the politics and inter-relationships of the organization. Service managers spend much of their time responding to questions, requests, and demands from supervisors and associates. They then communicate with their subordinates more than any other supervisorial position.

Operating supervisors are most involved with their own

small portion of the chain of command. They communicate with supervisors and subordinates more than with people outside the organization. Operating supervisors seldom have a picture of the whole organization and tend to be authoritarian.

Sales managers deal mainly with outgoing communication and may be somewhat isolated from the processes of the internal organization. Most of the sales manager's time is spent communicating with customers, clients, and competitors.

From this brief glance at different management functions, you may be able to gauge whether or not you are fulfilling your expected communications duties satisfactorily. Then you may measure how effectively you are using your time and where you can set aside more of it for yourself. General executives, since they are at the top of the hierarchy, have the most discretionary control over their use of time, but they usually work harder than anyone else and may not be able to distinguish work from play. They are the ones who most likely will not provide adequate time for thinking, relaxation, and interacting with people close to them.

## Major Time Losses

There is a long list of standard time wasters in the business world, but according to Ross Webber* and others, the major losses of time come from four fundamental problems: too much job; too much time; too much secrecy; and too much fear.

*Too much job* means just that. It is not unusual for a man or woman to struggle with responsibilities that are too dif-

---

*Ross A. Webber, *Time and Management* (New York: Van Nostrand Reinhold, 1972), p. 17.

ficult. Excessive demands lead to stress, distorted behavior, and wasting time. The person holding a job that is too big for him has inadequate time for reading and study, for internal inspection, and for visiting with subordinates. Above all, there are insufficient intervals of uninterrupted time for thought and contemplation. Many executives do not spend an hour alone each day.

The notion of *too much time* may seem contradictory, but it is not uncommon among mid-level staff positions. Such a person may urgently want to act but, in the absence of a real task or problem, may devote time to unnecessary activities. Such a person, responding to Parkinson's law that a job expands to fill the available time, may create unnecessary problems to solve. Overstaffing and excess time can also lead to hypersensitive human relations and personnel difficulties. The supervisor with too much time may overreact to normal situations, often calling excessive meetings involving too many people in too few problems.

Since, as we have noted, top executives tend to work the hardest, they then also set the pace for the office. Others work long hours to follow suit. As Ross Webber says, "The cafeteria and offices are sometimes filled with people who just feel they can't afford not to come in on Saturday."*

Restricted access to information needed to do a job is frequently a cause of wasted time. *Too much secrecy* is often caused by someone insecure in himself and/or his job. As a result, needless time is wasted in an effort to obtain information that otherwise should be readily available.

In fact, insecurity or fear is probably the major reason for wasted time. Originally, fear was a management tool to motivate lower class workers—fear of income loss, dismissal, and starvation. Although this tool may be wielded more subtly now, the middle manager often is more vulner-

---

*Webber, Time and Management, pp. 48–49

able to fear than ever. He may not be as afraid of dismissal, but he fears his failure to advance. That fear prompts a fear of losing status, and fear of losing control.

Once you see yourself and your position in the hierarchy of supervisorial jobs, determine whether or not you are subject to any of the four major time wasters. You may begin studying the time leaks that occur in your day-to-day activities, time that could be saved for creative procrastination.

## Time Wasters

There are two categories of time wasters—*external* and *internal*—the causes and potential solutions for both are within you.

External time wasters may include your superiors at work, your peers, or your subordinates. Although their claim on your time is primary, even members of your family may be guilty of wasting your time. The same is true of friends and acquaintances and telephone solicitors who intrude upon your privacy.

Consider a man in middle management who has been given an assignment. It may be a complex job requiring several days to complete. However, this man's boss comes in five minutes later with another assignment, and ten minutes later with a third. The boss feels *he* is getting work done but he doesn't realize that each time he pops into his employee's office, that man's concentration is disturbed. Each interruption delays completion of the first job. More time is lost because each time the subordinate gets another job, he or she becomes more confused about which task holds priority.

The rule should be that once you have received a task and the problem is made clear, no one has the right to intrude on your time (unless a problem is of overriding importance) until you are done. Obviously, you don't snap at your boss the next time he or she steps in the door, but in a polite, assertive manner, you can say: "It looks like this job will take me about two hours. I would appreciate getting the next one after this is done."

Or you can tell your boss that you would appreciate receiving all of the day's (or week's) assignments at once so that you can set up priorities and concentrate on each task in proper order.

This is one example of how you can *educate your environment* to reduce time leaks and schedule free time for yourself—while at the same time getting your jobs done more effectively. After recognizing how efficiently you work by controlling your own time, a boss should be happy to abide by your techniques. Countless hours can be saved by simple assertiveness, justifying the positively selfish desire to save valuable time for yourself.

The external time waster may be a civic leader who asks you to head a committee or collect for a cause to which you have little personal commitment. It may be flattering to be asked to do such things—and you may gain community prestige by doing so—but you must measure the value of your time against the intangible rewards. Time should be used in ways that give you the greatest benefit and satisfaction. Learning to say no without offending may be one of the greatest time savers of your life.

Internal time wasters are more difficult to eliminate because they involve mixed feelings about yourself. They are tied to insecurity, anxiety, lack of organization, and inability to make decisions. This leads to panic, emotional paralysis, and nonproductivity. Internal time wasters are linked with negative procrastination and usually involve unresolved conflict. The result is wasted time in which nothing happens.

It is relatively easy to be assertive and protect yourself

against strangers, acquaintances, or work associates. But it is more difficult to guard your time when you are intimately involved, as with spouse and children. If you come home tired from work and your son asks you to help him repair his motorcycle, what do you do? Most men would utter a frustrated sigh and half-heartedly help the boy. The son will certainly sense disinterest. It might be better to say: "Hey, I'm tired. Give me fifteen minutes to unwind and then I'll help you."

Although this example might seem to be an external time waster, the problem lies with the father's internal decision, or indecision, about the best use of that block of time. Usually the internal time leak mechanism is even more complex.

Ralph is an accountant and business consultant. He works at home and maintains an open-door policy with his wife and children. He remarked; "I don't have the heart to turn them away if they want something."

Because of this attitude—and because his work entails reading and paperwork and therefore does not *look* like work—his children pop in and out of his office at any moment of the day. Ralph's concentration is repeatedly disturbed. Even his wife assumes that he can absorb interruptions without impairing his ability to work. Again, even though the immediate source of time leaks are external, Ralph set up the situation internally because he could not say quietly but firmly: "I'm working from eight to five every day even though I don't go to an office. Before eight in the morning or after five in the evening, I'll be happy to give you my full attention, but between those hours don't interrupt me unless you have something important."

Most internal time wasters are unable to be assertive and decisive. They may even waste weeks or months rather than minutes or hours. Often they are people of high intelligence and sensitivity.

Tim, for example, was in his late 30s, approaching the peak of his successful career. He accepted many business commitments and was in high demand. He was a "nice guy," in the sense that he did not know how to say "no."

One of Tim's goals was to write a book related to his profession. The problem was that he had not set a high priority for getting the book done. He never found time for research, organization, and writing. He apologized to his editor because the manuscript was late, and he was frustrated because he failed to fit "book" time into his schedule.

Once he faced up to his "nice guy" personality along with professional realities and negative procrastination, Tim realized there were two simple solutions to his problem. He could assign the book a high priority and finish it. In so doing he would sacrifice instant gratification for long-term satisfaction. Or he could decide not to produce the book. This would be difficult because Tim wanted to write, and he abhorred leaving a task unfinished. This would, however, force him to honestly assess if it was possible to write the book in light of his other commitments. His reward, if he cancelled the book project, would be peace of mind. Tim would also learn that changing your mind is human, not weak. He would understand that when he *was* ready to approach the book again, he must give it high priority and proceed with it.

Tim suffered anxiety and embarrassment before he realized that writing the book was something more than just a "nice" thing to do. His pride prevented him from giving up, so he made room in his schedule and finished the manuscript.

The preceding examples may not fit your specific work environment and habits, but similarities should help you identify your own time wasters. Regardless of business or profession, a limited list of items emerges as the cause of most lost time.

## External Forces

Here are some examples of common outside forces which devour time wastefully:

1. The telephone. Do you accept all calls, regardless of what you're doing, or does your secretary screen, take messages and arrange a later time for you to answer the callers? Do you allow friends, and acquaintances to monopolize your time by phone, or do you set limits? Do you keep business calls short and to the point?

2. Meetings. When you call a meeting, do you insist upon an agenda and stick to it? Do you set a time limit, or let meetings run their course regardless of relevance? Are you drawn into meetings in which you have no legitimate function or at which you suspect little will be accomplished? Are you embarrassed to leave a meeting when you feel it is nonproductive? If you work in a group or team situation, it may be difficult to tell other people they are wasting your time. Polite assertiveness is the key. It may work best to call your team together and ask: "How can we all work together to eliminate wasted time?"

3. Interruptions. One way to maintain an open-door policy and still protect yourself against interruption is to establish a standard time of day for consulting others. A set time for talking with employees may turn into an informal group meeting, but it may be more productive than scattering appointments haphazardly throughout the day. Your subordinates *and* your boss should know when you are concentrating on an important problem.

4. Work conditions. Do you have enough light in your office as well as the proper work equipment? Is the noise level excessive? Everyone must adjust to working conditions, but if you do not have the proper surroundings, you should tell your boss that you could be more productive if your environment were improved.

5. The mail. Some people insist upon reading every piece of incoming mail. Others encourage their secretaries to screen the mail and deliver only those pieces which require action or reply. Which are you? Do you write or dictate letters whenever the mood strikes, or do you set aside a specific hour for this?

6. Incomplete information presented for problem solving.

7. Unclear objectives established by superiors.

8. Employees with personal problems.

9. Visitors.

10. Socializing in the office.

11. Poor filing system.

12. Deficiency of managerial tools or personnel.

13. Memo writing.

14. Poor communication.

The list of external time wasters could go on, but your exercise is to write a list of your own. Refer to your time log and continue to keep it up to date. In addition, write answers to the following questions: Which external time wasters are generated by *events*? Which are generated by other people? Which can I control or eliminate?

## Internal Time Wasters

As you go through your list and daily time log, you will find areas of lost time which cannot be accounted for by outside events or people. These areas point to your *internal* time wasters. These are some of the most common.

1. Lack of planning. Do you plan a project or do you just let it happen? Do you realistically estimate the time a job should require? Do you stick with your plan? Do your peers, superiors, and subordinates understand and concur with your plan?

2. Lack of priorities. Seldom do any two jobs hold the

same priority. Each day should begin with a firm priority list of things to do, remembering that eighty percent of the most important items can probably be done in twenty percent of the time. With such a list you will weed out tasks that can wait until tomorrow or next week, but be sure you are *not* postponing tasks because they are difficult or distasteful. If the priority list is followed diligently, you will find that important things are getting done more efficiently, with hours saved for creative procrastination.

3. Overcommitment. Attempting too much or having too many interests will result in confusion and time loss as you try to sort out priorities. Learn to say "no" and involve yourself in fewer activities at a time.

4. Negative procrastination. As discussed before, a job may be postponed because it is distasteful, boring, or difficult, and the tendency then is to linger over easy, routine jobs rather than addressing high priority work.

5. Indecision or postponed decisions.

6. Shuffling a piece of paper more than once instead of making a prompt decision about it.

7. Failure to delegate duties and authority.

8. Lack of self-discipline.

9. Lack of concentration.

10. Inconsistent actions.

11. Snap decisions that cause mistakes, forcing you to do the task again.

12. Poor communication.

13. Confusion caused by the mass of postponed work.

Again, this list is not complete because every person's habits and work processes are different. It will be useful to write down your own list of internal time wasters, taking care to be honest with yourself. As you compile your list, also try to establish how and why each time wasting habit crept into your routine.

Writing this list will be more emotionally difficult than

listing external time leaks because most of us are reluctant to confront our own failings. Remember, however, that the time you save is yours to use in pleasurable pursuits or for creative thought. You give these rewards to yourself.

## Time-Saving Ideas

To switch from looking at the negative, here are some positive time-saving ideas. Think of them as suggestions or guidelines, and apply only those that suit you personally. Any one of these ideas may be sufficient to improve your work effectiveness and provide free time. The objective is to perform your required duties in the least possible amount of time.

Time-saving ideas may be difficult to apply in work situations where an employee is expected to *appear* busy whether there is work to do or not, but this kind of job is degrading to the conscientious worker. Upper management should realize that if make-work situations or over-staffing exist, the manager has an opportunity to reduce staff or work hours, thereby increasing productivity and profits.

Some time-saving imperatives for the office might include:

1. Do not try to change your entire life at once. Begin with half a day at a time. Organize one morning a week toward better time use, then extend it to a day. Finally, plan your work (and play) schedule for an entire week. At first you may find keeping the time log and writing your plans time-consuming in themselves because you are starting to break entrenched habits. Soon, though, you will find the new techniques and processes becoming automatic.

2. Be aware of time. Think of your time as money and invest it wisely *every day*. Ask yourself frequently: "What is the best use of my time *now*?" When confronted by a major task, divide it into segments and estimate how long it will

take to do each part. Sometimes a flow chart is advisable as a graphic presentation of when the various components of the project should come together. Complete the parts in succession, following the time schedule you have estimated. The more complex the project, the better this system works.

3. Set priorities and stick to them. Some people are uneasy with the word "priority," thinking it requires a special sense or skill. It simply requires making a list of jobs every day, placing the most urgent and important at the top, and then working down through those less urgent. There is always enough time to complete important tasks. If you find yourself slipping into routine or "lazy" work, stop it and return to the high priority tasks. The fact that these may be difficult will enhance your satisfaction and self-esteem once they are done.

4. Estimate realistically. With experience you can estimate how long each job should take. Then assign ample time for it. If you think it needs an hour, allow an hour and fifteen minutes. If you finish ahead of time, reward yourself with the time left over. Have a cup of coffee or take a walk in the sun.

5. Select the best time of day for each kind of work. Each person has a natural rhythm which signals the most alert and productive time of day. It is up to you to examine your work habits, to become aware of when you do certain things best. Plan to fit your rhythm to the work at hand. Suppose, for example, that you are an architect or construction engineer. You are required to be in the office part of the day, preparing drawings and completing paperwork. During the remaining time you must be out in the field, inspecting the project. You may find paperwork interesting and stimulating in the morning but after lunch you are too relaxed and sleepy to concentrate. After lunch, then, is the time for your field trips—exercising in the fresh air and sunshine. Sched-

uling yourself this way can regenerate your body and mind in the afternoon, and you will accomplish everything more efficiently.

6. Do not over commit yourself. It's good to keep a busy office schedule, but reserve at least an hour each day of uncommitted time as a cushion against unforeseen events or for creative procrastination. This can be arranged by leaving ten minutes between each pair of appointments, or by freeing an hour in the middle or at the end of the day. If people crowd in on you, remember it is your time, not theirs. Few appointments are so urgent that they can't wait until later in the day or even until the next day.

This time saver also helps to ensure that one appointment does not spill over into the time reserved for the next one. You can control the length of most interviews; if you find that one is important enough to require more than the assigned hour, call and reschedule later appointments. How many times have you sat in a doctor's office waiting an hour after your appointment? This indicates that the doctor is overcommitted. Realistic scheduling gives you time to think about the next task and allows you to handle appointments efficiently without subjecting yourself to negative stress. People will respect you if you hold to firm schedules but are also able to give undivided attention to your caller while he is there. If time is left over between appointments, use it for other minor tasks or for relaxation.

7. Allocate time each day for planning. Planning should require no more than five or ten minutes in the evening or morning. Include your secretary or associates in the process so you don't spend the day reacting haphazardly to crisis situations. Time spent in calm, rational planning will pay off in work effectiveness. Try to find one new technique every day to help gain time, and this includes streamlining or eliminating old habits. If you know that your files are badly organized, for example, take the time with your secre-

tary to revise them. This will save more time later when you're searching for letters or documents.

8. Remind yourself of short- and long-term goals. Always keep in mind your objectives for what you wish to achieve this week, this month, this year, and for life. An awareness of goals will guide your work each day and help you to spend less time on trivia.

9. Use your waiting time. Many hours are wasted while waiting for the next event to occur. Keep a stack of small jobs at hand and do these while you're waiting. Or you may use this time for creative procrastination so that you will be sharper for the next appointment or event. Recognize the value of time spent in relaxation.

10. Find new ways to delegate duties and authority. Use your secretary and other subordinates to their full capacity. *Do not* cling to tasks because you believe you are the only person who can do them. Require *completed* work from your subordinates so that it doesn't need to be done again. Repairing mistakes and inadequate work are among the greatest time wasters.

11. Do not let paperwork accumulate. The person with the highest stack of paper in the in-basket may appear to be the busiest person in an organization; however, this sheaf of paper may also mean that person shuffles each piece several times before deciding what to do with it. The first time you see a letter or report, decide how to handle and *do* it. If someone else needs to do it, see that the paper gets to him or her promptly.

12. Keep meetings under control. Make sure the meeting is necessary; prepare an agenda and stick to it; see that the meeting ends at a specific time, and distribute minutes afterward so that all participants will retain the same message as to what transpired.

13. Control the telephone. Some managers welcome the intrusion of a phone call because it diverts them from a

distasteful job. But the telephone should serve its function and nothing more. Find out the purpose of the call quickly and resolve it promptly. Group outgoing calls together so that you can complete several in a short time. Before you place a call, be prepared to return immediately afterwards to the higher priority job you were doing.

14. Allow for crises and interruptions. You should anticipate unavoidable interruptions and occasional crises that must be handled. Time should be allocated each day for these purposes. Crisis management may be irritating but it may also teach you to save time by handling it better. Most office interruptions are initiated by a relatively small group of people. Manage these people by having your secretary screen callers to determine the nature and severity of their problem before admitting them. Before handling the interruption, make a note so that you will know precisely where to begin again on the work you were doing. Concentrate on one thing at a time; don't try to continue with your regular work while dealing with an interruption.

You can thus ensure successful time management by dealing with negative procrastination, by enlisting the cooperation of your associates, and by improving the time utilization of others in your organization. The final reward will be more free creative time for everyone.

# Time Savers at Home

Marilyn stepped inside the door of her house and kicked off her shoes in the same motion. *Lord, she was tired and her feet hurt.* Only as she collapsed on the couch did she become aware of the delicious odors emanating from the kitchen. Paul was home, cooking. And she was hungry.

The smell of food in preparation soothed her rumpled spirit. It made her feel secure as she had never felt secure in her previous marriage because she knew that she had found a relationship in which a man and woman shared the duties of life together.

She and Paul recognized that if each was to follow a career, they must help each other take care of housework in the most efficient manner, sharing burdens equally. In the same way, they shared the care and responsibility for two children—Sharon, 8, and Brent, 9—born of previous marriages but now living comfortably as brother and sister.

It was a successful arrangement as long as they stuck to their respective shares of the bargain: the first one home from work in the evening did the cooking, the other super-intended the children in cleaning up afterward. House-cleaning, laundry, and the myriad of tasks once considered woman's work were shared equally according to the job each person could do best—and *liked* best. It wasn't a per-fect arrangement but for the most part it worked. Marilyn saved time for Paul, he saved time for her, and they both saved time for each other. Saving time for creative procras-tination is just as important at home as it is in the nine to five business world.

## New Ways of Sharing

Until recent years, the working male presumed that most home duties would be taken care of by the "housewife." When he came home from work everything would be ar-ranged for his comfort and relaxation. Now more and more families fall into the category wherein both members of the couple contribute to financial stability. No longer can one member of the partnership be held responsible for all household chores. If a woman works all day at a job, she cannot be expected to come home and spend four or five more hours taking care of family and home. The division of labor between male and female is no longer as clearcut as it once was, and sharing family duties has become more important to joint happiness even when one partner does *not* work outside the home.

Awareness of this necessity in any family relationship is growing in our society, along with the other signs of liber-ated women. It is not only female, however, but also *male* liberation that is taking place. However, the latter is slower to take form because men remain dominant in conducting business. There are now three basic forms of household: the traditional marriage, in which the wife cares for home and children while the husband works to provide a living;

the dual-career couple which shares work both inside and outside of the home; and the working single who does not desire, or has not yet established, an exclusive relationship with another person.

A more unusual fourth situation also exists, that of the communal arrangement in which two or more men or women share a common household, each without direct responsibility for the financial security of the others.

Each of these relationship forms needs a specific pattern of time saving habits to allow an equitable sharing of free time.

## The Break with Tradition

The traditional marriage structure still exists in millions of households, but it is beginning to crack as husbands recognize it is not fair to hold their wives in serfdom, and wives feel the urge to explore their own varied potentialities.

The break with tradition can come in several ways: a husband may come home from his job prepared to take on his share of the household tasks and recognize his duty as a labor of love; or the wife may hold primary wage-earning power and the husband stay home to handle domestic tasks and child care. The important thing is to break the stereotypes of males and females so that they may work together in fulfilling duties and responsibilities. Each will then be a free individual and give free time to the other.

## The Dual-Career Couple

It is imperative that the dual-career couple recognize their interdependence and accept each other's right to personal and professional development. Some men feel threatened when a partner exhibits signs of greater professional ability than he, but this is a tendency that should be rejected. Instead, partners who work equally for common economic security and creative satisfaction should share equally the duties of home. This prevents either one from being over-burdened and helps to insure time for creative procrastination for both.

The man and woman in this relationship should share in planning for child care, in cooking and cleaning, and in making decisions as to who shall prepare breakfast, lunch, and dinner. One or the other probably will prefer certain duties and the chores can be divided in this way. In cases where preferences are not clear, the division of labor can rotate on a weekly or monthly basis.

The two must agree on how the children fit into the work pattern. They must also allow time for themselves as a couple, for themselves with each of the children, and for themselves with friends. If these factors are arranged in advance, the standard struggle between male and female stereotypes can be eased, if not eliminated entirely.

## The Working Single

The working single, man or woman, has no problem arranging time alone, but this person needs creative time to search out acquaintances, friends, and companions. The working single need feel no anxiety or guilt in creative procrastination, but must guard against negative procrastination as far as inviting friends for dinner or spending the night out are concerned.

If you live alone, don't avoid your home. You may prefer cooking short cuts, but you should be careful to eat nutritious meals. Necessary cleaning can be done on weekends or on an afternoon when you're expecting company in the evening.

## Saving Time at Home

1. Work smarter, not harder. Review your goals at least once a week and make them explicit enough to guide your daily activities. Make a "to do" list each day and place the most urgent and important tasks at the top. Look for new and shorter ways of doing things. Don't hesitate to experiment and innovate with routine work. You may unearth a gold mine of free time.

2. Schedule your time. Write appointments in a pocket or purse calendar. Leave some unscheduled time each day for unexpected events, such as friends dropping in for the evening. If it doesn't happen, you have a gift of extra time. Be realistic; don't schedule several large projects for the same day or you will be tired and frustrated when you fail to complete them. Schedule agreeable jobs between disagreeable ones. Promise yourself that you'll work on the car (which you enjoy) after you've mowed the lawn (which you hate).

3. Take time for yourself. Schedule time for yourself each day and *never* feel guilty about using it. Set aside a regular time for friends or for pursuing a hobby or sport. Have a place for retreat when you need to be alone. Carry a book (or whatever you like to do) with you so that if you are forced to wait somewhere, you can use the time productively. Experiment with reducing your hours of sleep to gain time for yourself in the evening or early morning.

4. Household chores. I have known couples whose homes were never clean or well-ordered but who seemed happy in the chaos of children, dogs, cats, and unwashed dishes. Others are compulsive house cleaners but are always tired and irritable with no time left to enjoy themselves. There is a happy medium between these two. Clean only what needs to be cleaned, promptly and efficiently. Delegate tasks to those who live with you so that everyone

does his or her fair share. Schedule an unpleasant job (such as rearranging a closet or cleaning the garage) one day a month so that you are not overwhelmed by the feeling that everything must be done at once. Challenge your imagination to find ways of doing each job in the least possible time.

5. Shopping. Use the phone directory and newspaper advertisements to save shopping and driving time. Buy in quantity to reduce shopping trips. Buy easy-to-care-for items such as no-iron clothes. Buy foods with minimum preparation time. Have a clear idea of what you want to buy before you go to the store—unless window shopping is your goal. Group a number of errands that can be done in one trip rather than dashing out for one item at a time. Planning and organization can save as much time at home as at the office.

6. Cooking. Plan menus in advance so that you shop only once a week and choose quick-preparation foods whenever possible. Prepare meals ahead of time and freeze for later. Use paper plates and cups, cooking bags, and foil to save cleaning time. These suggestions apply, of course, to the person who wishes to save time cooking. If culinary art is a labor of love, use it as creative procrastination and lavish upon it all the time and care you wish.

7. Entertaining. Keep convenience food and drink on hand for unexpected company. Give two parties on consecutive evenings since the house is already clean and the flowers arranged. An evening's entertainment planned for one group can serve equally well for another.

8. Socializing. If you want to see another person or family, make definite plans, and issue a specific invitation rather than leave it vague and ambiguous. Scan the Sunday newspaper calendar of events for interesting things to schedule for yourself and your family.

9. Grooming. Give up some television time to do regular exercise. Develop a morning routine that uses time to best

advantage, such as washing or shaving while the coffee brews and the muffins bake. Select the night before what you will wear the next day. Sell or give to Goodwill that closet-full of clothes you know you won't ever wear again.

10. Time with children. Set aside regular time to give undivided attention to each child. Have older children help care for the younger. *Expect* frequent interruptions. Train yourself to handle these and then return promptly to what you were doing. Don't insist upon total orderliness—picking up toys once or twice a week may be enough, *with the children's help*. Arrange car pools and mutual baby-sitting arrangements with neighbors and friends.

11. Handling paperwork. Have a special desk or place for all your household bills, checks, and correspondence. Set up a filing system and keep it up to date. Keep financial records carefully. Handle each piece of mail only once, unless it's a letter you enjoy rereading.

12. Other duties. Schedule yard work so that watering, weeding, and insect control are not all crowded into the same Saturday which you had wanted to use for creative relaxation. Maintain automobiles regularly to minimize road problems. Schedule major jobs, such as house painting, well in advance of the time when it will become a necessity.

13. Traveling. This is a time to enjoy and you should not be exhausted *before* you leave home. Make a checklist so you can pack quickly without forgetting anything. Keep a suitcase partially packed with basic items so that all you need to add are your clothes. On a short trip, use a suitcase small enough to fit under an airplane seat so that you don't need to wait for baggage delivery at your destination. If you are driving, allow plenty of time each day in order to enjoy the trip. Don't make an endurance test of miles traveled.

You should find that at least a few of these guidelines fit your specific needs for saving time and managing it effectively. You can establish a new time use routine when you keep your goals in mind, and realize you are saving time for your own pleasure.

CHAPTER

# How to Enjoy Creative Procrastination

If you experience difficulty in applying any of these principles and practices to your life, it is probably because one or more mental blocks stand in the way. In most cases the block that stops you from procrastinating creatively involves early life programming.

We are not trying to teach you how to be lazy. We are not teaching you to do nothing. Our overriding purpose is to help you learn how to *command and balance* the use of time to your maximum benefit.

It is not enough to make "to-do" lists and work hard all the time. You must also learn to schedule free time without feeling guilty so that during the rest of the time your work will improve and become more satisfying.

You must learn to say to yourself: "I want to do this because it will be beneficial to my business; because I want to make more money; because I will be more highly motivated to work. I'll be more successful and I will be healthier, mentally and physically. And I'll be a better husband, or wife, work associate or friend."

These are the motives, but you must also remove the mental blocks that subvert them. The primary stumbling blocks are:

Guilt feelings; inability to take maximum advantage of free time; measuring time only in terms of money; low self-esteem; nonproductivity; and catastrophic expectations.

## How to Overcome Guilt Feelings

Guilt is the most common and serious obstacle to balancing your life with creative procrastination. Engraved in our intellect and emotions is the message that working and producing is the okay way to live, but enjoying play and relaxation is *not* the okay way to live.

The first task, then, is to reprogram your thinking, your attitudes and emotions by giving yourself permission to schedule time for yourself. This requires building the confidence that you can accomplish what needs to be done while allocating free time each day.

Because you have been programmed by negative statements, write positive statements, such as: "I've worked hard today, so now I deserve some time for myself. . . I can take some time now because I know I'll work hard enough this afternoon to get things done. . . I can take off today because I know I can finish everything tomorrow or later in the week."

Writing these statements is important for two reasons. First, each time you do it you reinforce the positive impression, which is part of re-programming. Second, the act of writing confirms that you are *deliberating*, you're thinking and planning, not just drifting.

Note that it is not always necessary to work first and play later. Prime time is just as important for play and relaxation as it is for work. When I ask people when and how they procrastinate, they often reply: "I come home after work. Then I read the paper or watch TV."

Such people work hard until they are tired, and have no energy left either for work or play. This *is* one way you may use free time, of course, but it is at best a passive form of enjoyment. This is not a *creative* way to use time. Such people will not feel guilty but also they will not gain full satisfaction from the time because they are so fatigued. If you want to test this thought, try asking an acquaintance what show he watched on television last night. Frequently he will not remember.

Take free time when you want it, whether it be before or after a period of work. *You are in command of your entire time.* This is what it means to change your life style so that you are responsible for the balance between work and play. Your self-discipline is such that you need not feel anxious when you procrastinate creatively. As you begin to break the mental block of guilt, like yourself well enough to say: "How can I make this hour, or this day, very special? What do I want to do?" Perhaps you want to start the day playing tennis, or work in the morning and play golf or go sailing in the afternoon.

You may believe that the limitations of an eight to five job leave you no freedom, but you *can* program time for yourself in such work situations. You can plan it into your early mornings or in the evening. Only eight of the 24 hours are occupied by the job. There are times in the day, too, when you can daydream or fantasize creatively, going through the processes and detailed steps as though you have already done the job. The free-flow of day dreaming then reinforces the ease of getting into the task itself.

No one can say "my time is not my own." The time *is* your

own to use for making you happier and more productive.

Time planning and discipline may seem to be easier for the self-employed person, but it actually may be more difficult. Consider the doctor or lawyer, for example, who has spent years studying and training for his or her profession. Such people are strongly motivated. They feel compelled to schedule clients into every hour of the day and feel guilty if they don't. As one professional man commented: "Without considering anything else—my responsibility to mankind and all that—it's a matter of economics. My time is worth $50 an hour. If I don't earn it, I can't pay my office overhead and my family depends on that income. How can I justify taking time off?" This, unfortunately, is the common attitude that drives high achievers into ill health and early death.

Think for a moment. Do you really need to pack every moment full from nine to six? Why are you afraid to schedule a one- or two-hour appointment for yourself? Certainly clients and patients are important, but so are you. Suppose a physician told you that he could guarantee you an additional ten years of productive life if you would take an hour each day for exercise or relaxation. Would you believe him? Would you accept his *permission* to achieve this time balance for yourself?

## Redefining Values

If you feel guilty about the money represented by the hour you take off, consider the probability that what you're doing for yourself is more valuable. Redefine the value of the time you give yourself. Ask yourself these questions:

Why do I feel guilty about playing tennis, swimming, reading, or daydreaming? Do I believe it is a waste of time? Do I think I am being selfish and self-centered? Is it childish and egotistic to believe I deserve this time for myself?

The questions are negative. Create a new affirmative script for yourself, saying:

- I am going to be healthy.
- I am going to be productive.
- I am going to be happy.
- I am going to bring serenity and tranquility to my environment because I take care of myself.
- I am going to be a better balanced person because I take time for myself each day when I need it.

These positive statements are all part of goal setting. Keeping goals in view sets the framework for organizing time most effectively. The objective is to open the way for the extra dimension of creative procrastination so that at the end of each day you will feel more relaxed and fulfilled. This change of viewpoint and attitude will not happen instantaneously. You must practice and reiterate to change your behavior permanently.

Another tool to help accomplish this is the *affirmation statement*. Such statements are expressed in the present tense as though you had already achieved what you want to do. Here are some examples:

- I do not feel guilty when I take time for creative procrastination.
- I feel good about taking time for myself daily.
- I play tennis (or golf) every day for two or three hours.
- I take two hours every day for yoga and other relaxation exercises.
- I spend two hours every day with my hobby and I feel relaxed and enriched for doing so.

Several times a day say each of the things you want to do. Be in touch with your mind and body, and put yourself in a mental state where these things really are happening. At first you may still feel twinges of guilt, but as you repeat the affirmation statements (and do the things you promise yourself) you will create a new program in your mind. This will gradually replace the guilt which was associated with your past negative experiences and you will feel an upsurge of pleasant thoughts about yourself. Better health and higher productivity will confirm your decisions as you accept the value of creative procrastination.

## Learning to Enjoy Free Time

The astonishing fact is that most people simply do not know what to do with their free time, or how to use it for maximum advantage.

It's sad when we totally lose touch with the child in us that wants us to live for our own pleasure and satisfaction. We forget, or submerge, what *life* is about. We devote ourselves so single-mindedly to the tasks we must do, that we forget what turns us on, what gives us a high spot in the day. Men and women concentrate upon their jobs and are so fixed upon duty to others that they forget how to have fun. One man, for example, was troubled by his wife's complaint that they had little time to spend with each other. She accused him of "not loving me anymore."

"Doesn't she understand," he said, "that when I work long hours, that when I bring home the pay check, all of these are signs that I love her?"

In too many cases husbands and wives, as well as singles, have sacrificed and switched off the things they wanted to do for so long that they convince themselves they no longer want to do them. By constantly giving up personal desires and wishes, a person becomes dulled, reaching a point of not being stimulated by anything. He or she grows accustomed to a negative attitude about life in general, and this converts to chronic depression. Curing depression is one of the primary objectives in programming free time for pleasure and relaxation.

But what if you really do not know anymore what would give a lift to your day? What, for an hour, would lend a touch of excitement to a drab routine? (This is not to imply that all work is drudgery; it should be quite the opposite and a proper balance between work and play will help make it so.)

Just because you may not know what to do with the free time you create for yourself is no reason to waste it or do without it. Rather, you need to rediscover what will give you pleasure and satisfaction. You need to overcome the lethargy and depression which, through years of denial, have grown over your spirit.

## Listing Potential Pleasures

Clarify what you really would like to do by listing all those things that might give you pleasure. It isn't necessary to be sure they are all feasible or would necessarily give you satisfaction. Just let your imagination wander; you are not making commitments. If you can't think of things you know you'd like, perhaps include some your friends enjoy or you might enjoy together. Identify your own favorites. One caution: Do not turn off an idea because it now seems frivolous. Write it down so that you have a comprehensive list of things that might stimulate you in your free time.

Because your ability to enjoy events and activities may have grown rusty, try remembering things that gave you pleasure in the past and listing them: You're not little anymore, and your tastes have changed, but your life has been built upon past experiences. Perhaps some still apply. For example, a middle-age man was successful in business but distressed because he was unable to relax from work demands. He quickly grasped the principles for reorganizing his time, but then said: "All right, I can see how to take time for myself—quite a bit of it in fact. But what am I going to do with it? How do I use it? I've been revved up so long that I can't see how I'll use these extra hours. Do I stare at the walls?"

He might do that, of course, and he might be surprised how many creative ideas would flow through his mind. But he was also encouraged to remember some of his most satisfying pursuits from childhood. One of these was building model airplanes and cars. At first he rejected the idea as ridiculous, but one day he tried it and found he had submerged one of his greatest sources of pleasure. Now a room of his home is a small museum of original, detailed, and artistic models of ships and vehicles.

An attractive middle-aged woman who had achieved success in the business world found a balance by collecting antique dolls. One man turned to a childhood stamp collection and built it up for pleasure, therapy, and investment.

These examples illustrate why you need to remember how you once enjoyed using your spare time. Begin your lists by covering your elementary school years. In a second list, write down what gave you pleasure during your high school and college years.

In a third list, record the activities that refreshed your early working years. If you are married, list the things you enjoyed before you had children. The reason for writing the final list is that after you have children, you are burdened with responsibilities for home, husband or wife, and youngsters. During the years with a young family, you may forget how to take satisfying time for yourself because it seems impossible. That, of course, is when you need it most.

Traditionally, after marriage and first children, a man concentrated upon providing a good standard of living for his family. Wife and mother devoted her time and energy to housekeeping, child care, and answering her husband's needs. Although much of this may be gratifying in itself, in this pattern the husband frequently relinquished his earlier activities, such as hunting, fishing, sports cars, or sailing, because he felt he could not justify the time and expense. His wife detached herself from girlhood friends and solitary pleasures because there was no time for movies, museum trips, or relaxed afternoons browsing antique shops. After years of spartan devotion to duty, a yearning for pleasure may gradually give way to resignation and depression. This is why it is important to recall the fun things that once were different and exciting. And it is not enough just to remember. Relive them; close your eyes and meditate. Go back to the time when you danced or swam or practiced a hobby or wandered in the woods.

These lists now become your resource of spare time practices which once pleased you and might yet do so. Some of the things you enjoyed may no longer appeal to you, but others might be as pleasant now as they were in your youth.

As you go through the lists, pay attention to your emotions. Which activities bring back pleasant memories? Making doll clothes is out because you don't like sewing. But you never lost your love for music and it's not too late to return to the piano. Your art lessons were interrupted when you got married, but you still have the talent. Expressing yourself in this fashion might be exciting even though you have no illusions of becoming a master.

There is a wealth of possibilities for using free time to enliven your days and nights. Once you have identified some of these, try them, one at a time. And try them while listening to the emotional child in you. That child, who loved the world and the many things to do, is not dead, only hidden beneath the wrappings of work and duty.

I emphasize this point because there is also a danger, as you begin trying these once-pleasurable activities, that they will themselves become another burdensome chore. The adult in you may say: "I've started this thing and now I must finish it."

Explore the ideas and memories as a child, not as an adult. As you try an experience, take enough time to see if you like it or not. Don't drop out after the first experiment because one trial is not enough. Take the time to decide if this is something you will really enjoy during your hours of creative procrastination. If it is not, drop it.

For example, suppose you pay for a ten-lesson night course in wood carving but after four sessions you discover it's not for you. Drop it and move on to something else that will give you greater satisfaction and creative outlet. Let this intuitive and spontaneous child explore many avenues, but don't feel driven to stay with any of them if it isn't something you relish. Most people, once they stop feeling guilty for taking time for themselves, have little difficulty identifying rewarding ways to spend the time.

## Measuring Time in Terms of Money

Another mental block to creative procrastination is present in most people, but especially among high achievers. Professional men and women, successful business owners, corporate executives habitually equate time with money.

This, too, is a matter of conditioning. As we begin our careers we are paid a certain wage per week for our labor. As we progress, we expect the financial return to increase year by year. For the high achiever, this pattern continues until time is very valuable and hours are measured completely in terms of money. Time is a material commodity. For many men and women this tendency dominates the style of living until they cannot tolerate taking time for themselves.

This person needs to be more in touch with health,

strength, vitality, and diet, and realize as well that if he wishes to continue a successful life, he needs to take time for himself and his family—even if the time is worth $100 an hour. It is difficult for a successful executive to break this mental block. First, he or she needs to ask: "What are my material goals?"

Let's assume, for example, that the person has set a goal of accumulating $5 million in ten years. The next question is: "Why do I need $5 million? Is it to satisfy my ego, buy a palatial home, automobiles, yachts, and other possessions? Is it to satisfy my social aspirations or those of spouse? Is it to build an estate for children? Is it to acquire power?"

Each person needs to answer these questions honestly and evaluate the answers in terms of genuine satisfaction. The next question then is: What is the minimum level of wealth that would satisfy me? Write down what it would be for you. Perhaps you have already acquired nearly that much and, in re-evaluating your goals, realize you are already *there*.

Many people are already "there" in this sense, but they don't change their practices. Their internal computer is programmed to intense work, and they don't know how to turn if off. Momentum continues even though they've reached their objective.

One man said that he pushes himself at work because he enjoys it. Well and good. Work should be a joy. But when we delved deeper into his life, these facts emerged: He worked sixty hours a week without a break except for an occasional golf game. The foursome always included one or more clients, so golf was work time as well. This man took no time for hobbies or relaxation. He had withdrawn from his wife, whom he seldom saw, and she had learned to follow her own interests without him.

Such workaholics are more the rule than the exception.

For whatever reason, they are compelled to reach for higher material success even after they surpass their original goals. This person has several alternatives. He can reduce his work schedule to a thirty-hour week and still accumulate wealth, or he could spend half of each year traveling with his wife, expanding their intellectual horizons while enriching their marriage.

The rule of relative time values applies just as well to the person struggling to make a living for a family. For him the options are not measured in millions but rather in how hard he must work to pay his bills. A young couple, for example, might have as their goal the purchase of a new suburban home. The husband's salary isn't enough to accumulate a down payment. So they must decide if he will take a second job or if his wife will seek outside work. The decision hinges on the balanced use of time—should they sacrifice their free time, or postpone the dream. It is not an easy decision, but the value of free time wisely-used might well be greater than the new home.

The final question is this: If you already have your goal or see that you can reach it within one or two years, how will you use your time at that point to give pleasure?

The answer requires planning. It also requires you to decide whether you will continue working at top speed or if you'll take time for creative procrastination as you go along. If you can break the mental block represented by the success syndrome, you may not only enjoy life more now, but also enjoy it longer.

## Establishing Self-Esteem

Low self-esteem and guilt rank equally as inhibitors of creative procrastination. They feed upon each other.

Poor self-esteem causes you to judge yourself negatively in the fear that you are worthless, deficient, or unlovable.

Every person needs respect both from others and from himself. Unfortunately, respect from others and self-esteem are often confused. Many believe they can create self-esteem through other people, or from their environment, but this is not true. You can only give it to yourself. A person with low self-esteem is vulnerable and dependent upon how other people evaluate him. But the judges are themselves caught up in the achievement syndrome, and cannot judge objectively. The person with low self-esteem feels unable to take time off without risking the criticism and judgment of workaholic associates.

A man may seek material success as positive reinforcement from the world—assurance that he is okay—and a woman may compensate for low self-esteem by sharing her husband's success or by entering the professional field as a workaholic herself. However, no matter how productive and successful you may appear to those around you, the approval of other people can never suffice, in itself, to dispel an inner feeling of unworthiness. Only you can change this feeling.

As stated in *Positive Selfishness* by Porat and Quackenbush,* the roots of self-esteem lie in a lifelong process of being *aware* of yourself, *knowing* yourself and *liking* yourself a little better each day. These involve:

- Accepting yourself the way you are.
- Accepting yourself the way you want to be.
- Changing in a positive direction so that you will like your changing self even better.
- Accepting your body, the way you look, the way you move, the way you dress, walk, dance, talk, laugh, and cry. Your body is a statement of the choices you make about your life.

*Frieda Porat and Margery Quackenbush, *Positive Selfishness* (Millbrae, Cal.: Celestial Arts, 1977).

- Liking yourself as much as you like anyone else, feeling that you are *special*.
- Giving yourself permission to *be*. It is *your* responsibility to be happy.
- Accepting responsibility for building your own self-esteem. You are the only one totally committed to yourself.
- Learning how to make decisions and assert yourself. You are the sum total of your decisions and responsible for seeing them through.

The process of building self-esteem is active and continuous all your life. You must clarify values, goals, and priorities for your life, and be aware of the price you must pay for tradeoffs. You may have to give up friends to achieve privacy, or find you must be alone in order to fulfill creative urges. You may be forced to relax your money-making goals to have more time with your spouse and family. Make sure that the tradeoff decisions are in keeping with your objectives, and be sure to listen to different parts of yourself. They may push you in conflicting directions, but if you don't make an assertive choice, you will remain stagnant. Relinquish your past self-images. As a result of early experiences you may feel stupid, lazy, fat, ugly, and unlovable, even though you are no longer any of these—if, indeed, you ever were. Evaluate yourself fairly as you are *today*.

Do not expect instant breakthroughs. You are remaking a vital facet of yourself, so allow time for the process to work. Enjoy small achievements, and give yourself credit for small changes. Over a period of time, your self-image will change from that of a loser to that of a winner. As soon as you begin to feel that your actions and decisions are worthy and justified, you will reinforce such feelings through enjoying the free time you have earned and given to yourself.

# 8

# Eliminating Distress

A renowned investigator of the body's response to stress, Dr. Hans Selye, remarks: "Since stress is associated with all types of activity, we could avoid most of it only by never doing anything. Who would enjoy a life of no runs, no hits, no errors? Besides, certain types of activities have a curative effect and actually help to keep the stress mechanism in good shape."* Professor and Director of the Institute of Experimental Medicine and Surgery at the University of Montreal, Selye has spent forty years involved in laboratory research on questions related to pressure and stress upon the human mind and body. One of his primary themes is that since pressure and stress are unavoidable, the challenge is to convert them to our gain rather than attempting to avoid them. To do this, it is necessary to define the borderline beyond which stress becomes dis-

---

*Hans Selye, *Stress Without Distress* (New York: New American Library, 1971).

tress and to learn to control life just below that threshold.

It may be that contemporary society is prone to greater pressure and stress than any previous age. Pressure and anxiety seem to converge on us from every direction. The morning paper tells of higher taxes and inflation. Breakfast is spoiled by realizing that the dishwasher is broken. As you leave for work, you remember the car needs new tires and you're uneasy about a blowout as you thread through rush hour traffic.

At the office, the boss wants you to revise a report so your planned schedule is disrupted. All day you struggle to catch up with the work demand. As five o'clock approaches, pressure intensifies because the only way you can catch up is to work through the dinner hour.

You dread phoning your wife with this news because it has become an habitual pattern. She resents the loss of time and energy which she feels belong to her. On the phone she acidly reminds you that this also is the evening you had agreed to attend a meeting of United Fund executives. Out of pride and a sense of civic duty, you had weeks ago said "yes" to that volunteer job when it seemed your time would be less crowded.

So just when you should be able to anticipate a relaxed evening at home, you are torn by conflicting demands. In frustration, you dump the unfinished work into a desk drawer and stalk out of the office. You'll have dinner with your family and attend the United Fund meeting, even if it kills you.

And, if you continue to live this way, it could.

This picture of the middle level executive is not exaggerated. Such men and women are probably in the majority, the people who form the dependable structure of society. They are in their most productive years and run the highest risk of damaging their health.

The person who becomes so wedded to his job and the lure of success that he no longer shares time and energy with his family, is a corporate bigamist. Regardless of the personal or professional factors that push a man or woman in that direction, this person denies the spouse the soothing and healing pleasure of interpersonal relationship just as surely as if he or she engaged in an illicit love affair.

No matter how much professional satisfaction such a person derives from this perpetual "busy-ness," it is impossible to be away from home all the time without feeling anxiety, distress, and overwhelming conflicting demands. Such a person may be consciously or unconsciously avoiding unpleasantness in his home and marriage, but he also feels that he is drowning.

The answer: Take time to relax; reassess yourself, and seek a new perspective; and learn to play again.

That may sound simplistic. You may think of a dozen reasons why you cannot relax and play. However, if you do not learn to manage time well, you will always have difficulty relaxing. You will live under continual stress without a healthy balance in your life.

## Stress and Distress

We may have come to believe, at this point, that pressure and stress are automatically bad, that work and other pressures contribute to a number of degenerative diseases—as indeed they do if left uncontrolled. However, just as there is a distinction between negative and creative procrastination, there is an equally important line between stress and distress. As we consider ways to convert pressure to power, remember that it is impossible to live in our technical society without a certain level of pressure and stress; that level is necessary in order for us to accomplish anything. Stress becomes distress only when you are unable to control it.

Pressure can be a powerful force in your favor as long as it remains at a level where you can cope with it. If it surpasses your threshold of tolerance you feel frustrated and immobilized, and you suffer distress. This may be illustrated by two contrasting individuals. One is "Ms. Nice Gal," known as a glutton for work because she always says "yes" to anyone who approaches her with a task or problem. She agrees to attempt the most difficult projects because she has never learned to protect herself against unreasonable demands. She is afraid of what her superiors think of her, and seeks their approval by accepting any deadline, no matter how unrealistic it may be. Because she does not know how to assert herself, she absorbs the stress that continues to build as her work load increases. Although still relatively young, Ms. Nice Gal is a prime candidate for ulcers, heart disease, or nervous disability.

The other person is politely assertive. She knows and likes herself. She is no more skilled than Ms. Nice Gal, but she knows her subjective threshold of stress. She enjoys working under pressure but knows that if it passes the upper limit, her productivity will decline. She stops short of the stress level that will paralyze her, and if someone tries to push her beyond that point, she refuses.

It is perhaps obvious that this person will maintain better physical and mental health than the first. She will also command greater respect from her peers and superiors.

Here are some questions to help determine the level at which stress ceases to be a motivator and becomes distress:

- Do deadlines motivate you to work efficiently?
- How many simultaneous tasks can you cope with before you become confused and disoriented?
- Do you have the depth of knowledge needed to complete the projects?

- How much pressure can you tolerate from your superiors?
- How much internal pressure can you absorb without distress?

The questions can best be answered by relating them to recent work experience. Although fear of failure may encourage you to hide the facts from yourself, you *know* when the job situation really is too much. Once you have determined your optimum tolerance level, you are responsible for controlling your life so that level is not ordinarily exceeded.

It is not important whether you set your own deadline, or your boss tells you he wants the report by next Tuesday. The fact that a deadline exists is the motivating pressure to complete the job. No one will meet a deadline, or accomplish anything, without the healthy positive pressure of saying: "I should do this." A productive worker—on an assembly line or behind a desk—does not wait for his boss to come by and say: "All right, it's time to work now." Rather, the positive pressure to start work and continue working comes from within.

We cannot accomplish a difficult task or solve a problem unless we put all of our energy into it. Otherwise we'll be too relaxed and indifferent to convert stress into power and get the job done. Such indifference or lethargy leads to negative procrastination.

As a case in point, a young composer complained that he could not escape every day pressures long enough to concentrate on his music. George was confused by the conflicting stress of teaching, faculty meetings, and other university duties. He wanted to escape to focus on his creative work.

George eventually realized his dream. He was granted a winter sabbatical to write a concerto. He flew to Tahiti where he established himself in a comfortable, airy hut by the sea. He had no telephone, no television, no obligations to anyone but himself. The only people he saw were sun-browned vacationers and the islander who cleaned his hut and stocked his provisions once a week.

Long before his sabbatical ended, however, George was back from Tahiti. He was tanned, lean, and healthy, but his concerto was not finished.

"The place was perfect," he said. "I had comfort and beauty, and the sound of the surf was like a slow metronome. The first day I decided to take a swim before I got down to work. After that I took a nap. In the evening I wandered down the beach to town and spent half the night watching people in a bar. I'd get to work tomorrow.

"The rest of the story is classic beachcomber. I didn't have any pressure to teach or pay bills so each tomorrow melted into another. I convinced myself that one day the inspiration would strike and then I'd get to work. It never did.

"Then one day I got a letter from my publisher, a light note hoping I was having a good time and incidentally asking about the music. It was the spur I needed—just that hint of pressure—and that day I decided to fly home and get to work."

## Stress As a Motivator

George's example is not typical because few of us are composers, artists, or writers waiting for the muse to call. Not many people can arrange a paid vacation in the South Seas to escape the stress of living and working. However, the lesson is the same: whether our job is teaching, office work, practicing law, or supervising a corporate division, we all need a certain level of pressure to motivate achievement.

One way to manage stress so that it becomes an energizer

rather than demoralizer is to set up your own pattern of pressure, by becoming your own source of *reward and punishment*. Control your time and environment rather than allowing them to control you. You can create an artificial situation by saying: "I'm going to finish that report by noon today," even though it isn't due in your supervisor's office until tomorrow. Set up personal privations and rewards to go with the deadline, such as: "If I don't finish the report, I'll work through the lunch hour and I know I don't like to miss lunch."

Self-imposed pressure provides not only the impetus to finish the job but also, of avoiding the more severe stress of the boss's criticism. Doing a good job also builds confidence that you will do as well or better next time. This can be a powerful tool in managing time and scheduling creative procrastination for yourself each day. Rather than waiting for the ultimate deadline on any job, plan ahead so that you gain command of tolerable surges along the way, keeping the overall pressure below the distress level.

## Reconditioning Your Responses

Generally speaking, we dread pressure. For people who live and work under continuing high-level stress, often only a small increment of additional pressure is enough to throw them into panic or illness. We know that excessive stress can be destructive. It is associated with ulcers, vascular problems, and psychosomatic ailments in general. Thus, most people are reluctant to face stressful situations. A new challenge appears as a negative rather than positive opportunity for growth.

Because of this conditioned response, many people give up too easily on a problem. When confronted by a stressful situation, they become frantic, weak, and incapable. Their energy drains away into negative feelings of hopelessness.

The task, then, is to recondition attitudes toward pressure and accept it as a positive force. This will not be easy for the person already laboring under a stress overload, but by first working through small problems you will gain the power to accept and cope with harder situations.

For example, Gordon was almost literally paralyzed when asked to address a group of people. He was a competent aerospace engineer and had been invited to present a paper before a meeting of his professional society. The convention was months away but he was already suffering stage fright.

Gordon was advised to practice before less important audiences before approaching the greater challenge. He joined a Toastmasters Club and within a few weeks began building confidence in his speaking ability. When the convention date arrived he was still uneasy but did not allow the stress to overwhelm him. After the speech several people congratulated him on the clarity of his delivery.

Instead of fearing stress, think of it as an opportunity. For some people, the greatest accomplishment of their lives was confrontation with and victory over a situation that threatened comfort or security. One woman had established a successful extension course at the state university. The study series was well-attended and popular but one day the dean advised her that economic problems probably would force cancellation of her course the next semester.

At first she was depressed by the impending loss of teaching exposure and income, but she asked for a hearing to present her arguments before the final decision. She approached the meeting anxiously, but also with well-prepared information. Her presentation was so forceful that the course was retained in the extension schedule.

"Stress was a tremendous motivator," she said. "It gave me inner strength and excitement. I found out there is almost always an alternative way to convince people or to resolve a problem."

In reconditioning response to stress, an unknown or frightening situation thus becomes an opportunity and a new beginning.

## Stress Tolerance

Sometimes people are overwhelmed only by stress created by a specific kind of situation. For instance, a person may be afraid of water. His tolerance threshold is zero at the ocean or swimming pool, so he does not swim. For someone else, tolerance to water and swimming is high and causes no stress at all.

Here is a quiz to help you determine your tolerance to stress from three sources: internal, interpersonal, and environmental.

In answer to each of the questions, estimate your tolerance level from zero to five, zero indicating severe anxiety or fear and five the level at which you feel no pressure or stress:

*What is your tolerance to noise?*
- To noise of children?
- To other people talking?
- To rock-and-roll music?
- To highway traffic?
- To motorcycles and machinery?
- To jet planes?

*What is your tolerance to danger?*
- Do you gain a thrill watching, or participating in, dangerous sports?
- Are you afraid of swimming?
- Of horseback riding?

- Of freeway driving?
- Of auto or motorcycle racing?
- Of flying?
- Of mountain climbing?

*What is your tolerance to deadlines?*
- Are you stimulated or frightened by a single deadline?
- By several deadlines at once?

*What is your tolerance to public speaking?*
- Does an audience frighten you, with or without a microphone?
- Do you expect and enjoy audience participation?
- Do you avoid public speaking at all costs?

*What is your tolerance to argument?*
- To conflict with business associates?
- To argument in a social discussion?
- To criticism from a friend or acquaintance?
- To your wife or husband's anger?

*What is your tolerance of a heavy work load?*
- To difficult tasks?
- To unpleasant tasks?
- To boring projects?
- To projects that require creative thought?

*What is your tolerance to catastrophic expectations?*
- When you leave home, on vacation or weekend?
- On the highway?
- When the telephone rings?
- When the mailman comes?
- When the doorbell rings?
- When a telegram or special delivery letter arrives?

*What is your tolerance to uncertainties or ambiguities at work?*
- Do you wonder what other people are whispering about?

- Do you play office politics or avoid it?
- Are you concerned about someone being "after" your job?
- Are you uneasy or anxious when the boss calls you into his office?

*What is your tolerance when things go wrong?*
- When a check bounces?
- When you lose your billfold and credit cards?
- When the checkbook is not balanced?
- When a household appliance needs repair or the roof leaks?
- When the car breaks down during a journey?
- During an emergency at work?

*Are you aware that you have any phobias?*
- Fear of heights?
- Fear of closed rooms?
- Or open spaces?
- Fear of crowds?
- Or of being alone?

After defining your stress sensitivities, analyze each one. For example, Why do I sense danger in certain situations? Are they really dangerous? Why do I feel this way about an unpleasant task? Why do I anticipate unpleasant news when the telephone rings? Is it because I have failed to perform some duty and I'm afraid someone is calling to criticize? Do I dread the mailman because I haven't paid my bills?

As you study each item, be alert to those stress points you may be able to eliminate. Often we build unjustified fears about unreal situations. Facing them squarely can remove them. A candid exchange of views with your boss may clarify both your expectations of the other and ease your fear of criticism. Most pressures can be converted to positive challenges; reducing stress to manageable proportions can give a great sense of relief.

## Power Checklist

Once artificial or false stress points are placed in proper perspective, you are in a better position to cope with legitimate pressures which can unleash your powers of concentration and performance. By following this checklist of steps you can gain power and confidence from unavoidable pressure.

Take one thing at a time. Your work load may seem unbearable, causing you to feel trapped and confused by the number of things that need to be done at once. Select several of the jobs that are easiest and clear them out of the way promptly. While you are doing one thing, don't worry about the next. As you complete each item, your tension will ease and the sense of accomplishment will reinforce your strength for the next one.

Organize the pressure. This goes hand in hand with number one. Take the time to analyze your job, sorting out tasks that are urgent *and* important, rather than just urgent.

Learn to equalize your stress. Alternating pleasant and unpleasant tasks will provide variety in your everyday life.

Take a breather now and then. Change your position. If nothing more, stand up at your desk. Inhale deeply and let your breath out slowly several times. Stretch and exercise your upper back and shoulders. Slump in your seat from time to time and clear your mind of immediate problems.

Change your routine. Go to a different restaurant for lunch, or carry your lunch with you and spend the noon hours relaxing. Walk instead of riding to and from the station on your way to work.

When you arrive home, take a brisk walk or other exercise. Exercise is the best way to dissipate the excess adrenalin that has built up in the blood during your pressurized day. Take a hot bath and retire early.

When you rise in the morning, tell yourself that you will

derive strength and high performance, rather than fear and anxiety, from the day's pressures. The gradual but satisfying conversion of pressure to power will begin to emerge. Each success will strengthen and reconfirm your ability to tap this reservoir of energy.

# How to Plan Your Life

There is no need to continue following your old negative life scenarios. You can initiate a new approach to life today. Your new life style will start the hour you begin. This chapter moves beyond day-to-day considerations to focus on planning your entire life as part of a time management program. If you really know what you wish to achieve, then you can concentrate your energy and resources on actualizing those goals.

Many people drift through life, permitting their actions to be governed for them through other people's opinions (parents, teachers, bosses and spouses), or through circumstances ("I must take whatever job is available because I fear insecurity").

Certainly everyone is influenced by external forces; we cannot avoid this nor, in most cases, would we wish to. They help guide us. However, there comes a time, at age eighteen or seventy-seven, when we must take control and assume responsibility for the way we spend our remaining days. We cannot wait for fate to push. If you have studied the preceding chapters, you should be ready to expand your horizons beyond tomorrow and next week, and to plan your life for the greatest possible achievement which allows free time for yourself and maintains mental and physical health.

## How Much Time Do You Have?

Obviously, no one can answer that question. During this century average life expectancy has been increasing (by virtue of lowered infant mortality and better control of infectious diseases) until the average life expectancy of a child born today is anticipated to be above 70 years, and even more for women.

However, no one is average. You might have fifty years left, or you may die tomorrow. Nothing we have said about managing time for creative procrastination and improved health guarantees an increased life expectancy, but the practice of these principles will certainly improve your odds. We would be well-advised to follow the attitude of the man who said: "I never think about dying. For all I know, I may live to be a hundred."

But what, then, is a long life in terms of achieving goals and wishes?

Some people achieve professionally and gain wealth by age thirty or forty. Others may continue trying to age eighty and beyond without ever achieving what they most wanted to do. Some apparently successful people never reach the success they once visualized for themselves.

One man, for example, became a physician because his parents and teachers urged him to go to medical school, but his deepest desire was to be a concert pianist. Another wanted to become a forest ranger but, because his family was poor and he feared insecurity, he spent most of his vigorous years as a salesman. He was a good salesman and successful in the material sense but he never satisfied his deepest yearnings. A woman who studied interior decorating allowed her profession to languish so that she could care for her home, husband, and children.

These are some examples of why it is important—no matter what you are doing now or how old you are—to plan the use of your remaining time in the most profitable manner. Profitable means satisfying your goals and needs, not necessarily money or material possessions, although these may well be part of your objective.

Whether you are young or old, your remaining time is precious. It is sobering to realize how short a lifespan may be in the flow of time and history. If you were to live 100 years, you have 36,500 days from birth—876,600 hours, or 52,602,000 minutes. The minutes pass whether you do anything with them or not. If the hours were dollars, you would think very carefully about how to spend them. Actually, the hours are even more precious than dollars. You need to control them, to take responsibility so that the time left in your future will serve you most pleasurably and wisely.

## The Past As Guide

How do you start planning your future? *Let your past be your guide.*

You can plan intelligently for the future only by examining your past to determine where, when, how, and why you used time well or badly. You may find that you used it to your complete satisfaction, but you may also uncover examples of negative procrastination which thwarted the achievement of your goals.

It isn't enough to wander vaguely through your memory; recall must be precise. It will help to break your past life into units of perhaps five or ten years each, and examine each unit. Go as far back as you can remember any sense of responsibility for the use of time, perhaps when you started school. Now, on separate sheets of paper, begin writing two lists.

The first will include occasions in which you *now* feel you had mismanaged time to a degree that it caused trouble with other people—parents, teachers, or employers—or trouble within yourself. The former might include negative procrastination when you should have been doing assigned chores or an important job. The latter includes occasions, or behavior over a period of time, that resulted in internal conflict, difficulty, pain, guilt, or frustration.

The second list will include pleasant highlights of your life in terms of time use. Remember how you did something exactly the way you wanted to and were pleased with yourself or received good feedback from others.

One farm boy, for example, spent hours each summer day throwing a baseball at a target on the side of a shed because he had no one with whom to play catch. His father chided him for taking time from his farm chores, but the boy continued practicing to achieve throwing accuracy. Later he became one of the best pitchers on his high school baseball team.

As you write your two lists think of negative and creative procrastination, how the former wastes time without result, while the latter increases your creative power and productivity. Think also of *why* you used or misused time the way you did and analyze your feelings about it both then and now.

Perhaps one of your sharpest memories relates to school years when you delayed homework until you were forced to do it. Write down why you hated homework. Was it the subject matter? Was it because you wanted to play with friends? Perhaps your teacher was disagreeable or you postponed homework just to spite your mother because she nagged you. Do you now regret that you didn't study harder, or is this example of procrastination a happy memory? What feelings did it give you then? How do you feel about it now?

When younger you may have enjoyed arithmetic while despising history and social studies. As a result, you spent all your time on math and slighted the other subjects. Although you failed history, your love of math later led you to a successful career in that field. In this case, the procrastination should go on your positive ledger because your behavior finally led you to a happy result.

On another occasion, when you were eight, your mother hired a piano teacher to give you lessons, even though you wanted to learn the guitar. Both your mother and teacher insisted that the piano would give you a better music foundation and forced you to practice every day. Instead of practicing, you dawdled until your daily time in bondage ended. Finally, after two years, your mother agreed the lessons were a waste of time and money and allowed you to quit.

Think about this. What did you get out of it? Did you feel a sense of triumph, or were you simply trying to gain your mother's attention? Do you now regret that you didn't continue with music? Do you feel that you may yet study piano?

Perhaps when you were young you were sloppy about tidying your room, thus making your parents angry. Again, recall what you gained or lost by this behavior. Were you asserting your independence, or testing your parents to find out how much disobedience they would tolerate? It may be that you felt good about not cleaning your room and still feel good about it today.

This illustrates the point that you are now the only judge of how you used or abused time in the past. You may remember some time-wasting experiences as painful and negative, others as positive and satisfying. You may have been punished for the day you cut school, but your memory of the day is: "Wow, it was wonderful to sit up on that hill with the warm breeze blowing in my face."

It is essential to use time well and productively but also important to be in touch with the mischievous and creative parts of yourself, the free spirit that lived and still lives in you. Some things you have done might meet with general disapproval, but if you feel okay about them they should be listed as positive experiences.

Continue both lists, through high school and college. Did you date girls and go beer drinking with buddies while you should have been studying for exams? Did you drop out of the university to hitchhike and bum around the country? Suppose, while you were wandering, you were forced to take a job pumping gasoline in a service station in order to eat. After that, the line of least resistance seemed to be garage work and mechanics. You postponed your fading desire to complete work for your degree.

How do you feel *now* about that? Do you believe that your year of wandering was more valuable than a year of college? Do you feel your life would have been better if you had obtained a degree quickly? Do you feel that it is still possible to return to the university?

As you recall events, be alert for habit patterns of time use which repeatedly caused frustration or difficulty as your life progressed.

When you obtained your first job, were you punctual or frequently late to work? Did you plan and execute your work efficiently or did you loaf at the water cooler while the boss was out of the office? Did you need repeated reminders to complete a job? Were your salary increases and promotions delayed because of such habits? Possibly you were once fired because of wasteful time habits, although your employer gave you another reason at the time.

Be completely honest with yourself. Write down everything that comes to mind, even if the memory is painful.

These lists are not for the purpose of atoning for past errors, but for identifying those areas of time mis-management that slowed your development and prevented you from reaching your goals.

But do not spend time *regretting* the past. Almost everyone has made mistakes. It is a useless exercise to dwell morbidly on missed opportunities or on "what might have been." The life inventory is strictly for pin-pointing those habits which hampered your progress and to assess whether or not you have improved in the intervening years.

Bring the lists up to the present time and then identify the things you are doing now that are obstacles to living a holistic life and managing time in a healthy way.

Through your self-inventory and the skills taught in previous chapters, you now have the knowledge to do it right. You have the tools to create a future incorporating time management, ways to procrastinate creatively without guilt, how to use stress in a positive and regenerative way, and how to deal with the elements of physical well-being and mental health. You know how to take responsibility for your use of time, for good nutrition, for daily exercise, meditation and relaxation. What remains is to do it.

## Plans and Ambitions

Almost all of us set goals for our lives: "by the time I'm twenty-five, I want to be a successful engineer"; "by the time I'm thirty I want to own a farm"; "when I'm forty I want to be independently wealthy"; or "at sixty I want to retire and travel around the world."

No matter how vague your personal and professional desires might have been when you were young, you had some life ambitions and deadlines for fulfilling them. Whatever your age now, if you have not approached fulfillment of your goals, you will be frustrated and depressed until you revise your objectives. You may find that your original aspirations were unrealistic or that life conditions changed beyond your control.

For example, what happens if a person puts money in the stock market with the ambition of becoming a millionaire by age forty, but the stock market crashes? He cannot realistically stick to his original plan because conditions have changed. Another person studies to become a dentist but after ten years of practice finds that he doesn't like it. A woman whose ambitions were to practice law falls in love and gets married. She is frustrated because her profession is sidetracked.

Some people spend most of their lives pursuing goals which were unattainable for one reason or another. They must take into account changing conditions, as well as altered desires and abilities, and adjust goals accordingly. It is not enough just to drift. There must be a positive and decisive shift in direction. Odd as it may seem, the same need to shift aspirations applies to the person who runs ahead of his original plan. If you have gained the affluence that was your original objective, how will you use your wealth and, more pointedly, how will you use your future years productively?

On the other hand, let us suppose you're doing poorly in your job, probably indicating you are not well-suited or trained for what you are doing. Feeling unproductive, you become unhappy, anxious, and bored. This is not the best use of your time. If you manage well, every day should give you satisfaction at work.

The same is true of personal relationships. If you're in an unhappy marriage, you're wasting those precious days of your life. If you are unhappy at work or in marriage, write into your master plan ways to change the use of time so that life is more pleasant, satisfying, and productive.

Regarding work and its rewards, you may be able to map

performance improvements that will lead to advancement or a better position within your company. However, if you're at an obvious dead-end, do not hesitate to consider a change in company or even career.

## Changing Course

As life expectancy increases, our working lives also extend, to perhaps forty or fifty years. It would be unusual for one profession or occupation to absorb and excite a person consistently for that many years. As a result, it is increasingly common for men and women to change careers during their lifetime. This trend is facilitated by the growing popularity of continuing education through which people can re-educate themselves for new occupations.

Mac, for example, was department manager in a firm which manufactured electronic components. Although his peers considered him successful, he was unhappy. His uneasiness manifested itself in gastric ulcers and other distress symptoms. Mac revealed that he had lost interest in the goals he had set as a young man.

"For years I wanted to run my own company," he said, "but now that I might have a shot at being president, I don't want it. I feel that I *should* want it, but I don't. I'd really like to operate some resort cabins in the mountains. It would clean out our resources," Mac added hesitantly, "but we could do it. I haven't discussed it seriously with my wife. It's one of those things you dream about. But I think she'd be willing to go along with almost anything that would snap me out of my miseries."

Mac grew excited as a dream began to assume genuine potential. He knew how to get the knowledge he needed, and was willing to spend the time to train himself. Shortly thereafter he bought his string of cabins in the Wyoming Rockies.

## Change As Motivator

More often a person lacks the resolve to change career course. Another man took an educational short cut after World War II. He wanted to be an aerospace engineer but, because the hours of study were shorter, became a teacher instead. For the past 20 years he has been principal of a large midwestern high school but he has no prospects for advancement and hates what he is doing. He feels too old to change and fears taking the time to train himself for another career. This man is bitter, and realizes that he is wasting his life, but he probably will do nothing about it.

Some people do not comprehend why they are unable to deal with reality. They are aware only of an unpleasant feeling that things are not going well. They dread getting out of bed to face a new day. They are not motivated and, indeed, are no longer trying to succeed. This apathetic condition may relate to the person or professional side of life, or both. Ask yourself some questions to sort out confusion and depression, and identify a beginning point for change. Answer honestly to define where you are and where you would like to be.

First, regarding work:

1. Do you feel that your difficulties are your fault or due to your environment?
2. If you are at fault, is it because you have not gained mastery over the use of time?
3. If work environment is causing the difficulty, is it because the job is too hard? Too easy?
4. Is your uneasiness caused by personality conflicts with your associates or your boss?
5. Do you believe your salary is inadequate or that you should be promoted?

6. Do you think you can change the situation or are you convinced you must look elsewhere for a job?
7. Do you feel that you need to change careers? If so, what would be your choice of new direction?

Take special care with the last two questions. Do not make hasty decisions. You may need only to concentrate on one aspect of work and discuss it candidly with your superior to effect an improvement. You may be able to accomplish the necessary change internally without shifting careers, but you must be positively selfish and assertive. Say to yourself: "My time is valuable. Unless I express myself, other people cannot know what I need."

Delineate clearly what you want, then speak up. In doing so, you may improve the situation. If this straightforward approach fails, then you may think of changing jobs or career.

## Personal Change

This is neither the time nor place for a course in marriage counseling, but if your difficulties are with spouse and family, a few more questions may help to clarify those problems as well:

1. What is the greatest source of conflict between you and your spouse?
2. Does he or she know how you feel about this?
3. Do you communicate clearly, frankly, and assertively with each other?
4. If not, are you willing to improve, to take the time to talk things out candidly and rationally?
5. Are you willing to expose hidden grievances in order to improve your marriage?
6. Do you believe your marriage has gone sour because of your unhappy work situation? Or vice versa?

7. Can you change your family or marital situation internally?
8. Do you feel, after careful study and deliberation, that separation is your only answer?

Major decisions are never simple and therefore it is advisable to consider all questions carefully. Give yourself time for logical, unheated thought. Opting for divorce during the stress of argument may be the wrong marital decision.

On the other hand part of your occupational problems may stem from the fact that you live alone and spend your nights seeking fun and companionship. You feel no sense of personal commitment or motivation because you have no one to love. Your crisis then may be the decision to marry a person who will give you a feeling of purpose.

## Life Transitions

You may find, as many do, that when you have done something positive to reorder one part of your life, other aspects will improve also. Sometimes, however, a major change in career or personal relationship is necessary to prevent wasting the rest of your life under unsatisfactory conditions. Sometimes the change comes at work, sometimes with family, sometimes with both. If you decide that you have come to a major transition in life, understand also that during the period of change you are unusually vulnerable and susceptible to stress. This is the time, above all others, to be kind to yourself.

Try to make major shifts one at a time; don't unsettle your career, your marriage, and place of residence all at once. Be in touch with your stress tolerance level. A time of crisis is when you should take *more* time for yourself, work slowly and deliberately, take care of your body and indulge yourself. If you are moving from one job or career to another, your spouse must be informed and should concur with how and why you are doing it. Your spouse also will suffer stress but this can be an occasion for greater warmth and closeness if you take the time to be considerate to each other.

Once you have decided upon a major transition, schedule enough time to prepare for the change. Set a goal and take time to learn whatever is needed to achieve it. For example, an electronic engineer might wish to be a high school math teacher. His knowledge of math is adequate but he must plan a year to take education courses for a teacher's certificate. A woman returning to the business world after her children are grown should allow relaxed time for refresher courses and to talk with others who are currently in the occupation. An auto salesman should not shift abruptly to real estate without studying specific techniques unique to his new venture.

Allow time for learning new things, meeting new people, and maintaining a balanced life-style while you do it. A person caught up in crisis may neglect health or family and friends. You must be aware and create a balance or you will never find time for the most important things in life.

As you plan your future years, allow also time to adjust to the unpredictable. Unexpected events—the death of a loved one—are a natural, though often painful, part of life. Allow for them to happen. It is often necessary to shift priorities as circumstances change.

Be methodical about moving into a major new project or situation. Collect the knowledge you need and then, once you are confident that the goal is sound and attainable, you won't need to spend energy worrying about it. Use the energy to enjoy your creative procrastination.

While it is important to set long-term goals and pursue them, you also need to remember this: *There are few end results in life, but many processes.*

Learn to enjoy the process, such as children growing up, rather than anticipating when they will leave home for college or marriage. Enjoy the process of landscaping your home, instead of dwelling on the day when it will be perfect and you can sit and look at it. Nothing is ever quite perfect, so the ultimate goal is to outline the processes that will give you greatest personal and professional satisfaction along the way.

As you put these planning lessons to work, continue to keep in mind the basic principle for time management: you cannot live well unless you allow time for yourself. This may now mean more than a few minutes or an hour a day; it incorporates realistic long-term planning. Learn to respect and like yourself. Develop confidence and self-esteem so that you know you can achieve whatever you set out to do; you have many options and the right to choose the ones that will be satisfying, relaxed, and healthy. Make time work for you rather than against you; you have the right to take time for planning and meditation so that your working hours are more effective. You have the right to plan your life and live the plan.

# 10
CHAPTER

# Review and Commitment

A person who is happy views life as a succession of chosen activities and manages time with the deliberate intent of allowing intervals of pleasure and *nondoing*. This is the key to keep in mind as you make a new contract with yourself to reprogram methods and attitudes toward the use of time.

Psychological well-being is intimately connected with a sense of control over life and a purpose in your undertakings. Adroit management of time helps to achieve this by imparting that sense of order, accomplishment, purpose, and control. Finally, proper time management, which incorporates creative procrastination, is a tool which allows you to be more relaxed and effective in everything you do.

Some people have difficulty translating general ideas into specific practice. Self-assessment questionnaires and exercises have been included to help you with this translation. It may also be helpful to see how others have struggled through some questions and statements more frequently encountered in seminars on creative procrastination. Finally, you will be challenged to make a new contract with yourself toward effective use of your time.

## Questions and Answers

*How do you define procrastination?*

Most people define it negatively, as a wasteful misuse of time. This definition is correct *only* for negative procrastination. More pertinent are these questions: who says it is bad to take time for yourself; why is it evil to do nothing; and why must we finish a job immediately?

You are the judge, and managing time means managing yourself. Creative procrastination is deliberately programming free time as part of your schedule, whether it be a few minutes in the day or a four-month cruise around the world. You know how you are going to use the time and enjoy it. You know that your self-awarded freedom will stop at a certain hour and then you will go back to working more effectively as a result of having taken the free time.

*What are suitable activities for creative procrastination?*

Whatever feels right to you. If your job requires developing new ideas, you might choose an activity for free time which does not demand analytic thinking or effort. If your job is sedentary, you probably would choose physical exercise to relax and re-energize. A person in a boring and repetitive occupation might want to study music or art, something that poses a creative or mental challenge. Most people seek diversity.

*What makes creative procrastination pleasant?*

First, you have presented this time to yourself as a gift; do not feel guilty about using it. Second, during this time there should be no feeling that something must be completed. Some have said that during their free time they prefer doing what they do best to build ego or self-esteem. Some speak of tennis, others of gardening. If you are already good at something, this time may be spent improving that skill.

One woman had suffered polio as a child and was partially handicapped, but she said: "What I can do well is swim." She used her free time to improve her aquatic ability. Now she swims with a snorkel and can relax in the water for hours, suspended in a state of mind and physical being resembling meditation.

*What if I have trouble sticking with my creative procrastination activity?*

If the activity is difficult or unpleasant, then it is *not* creative procrastination. Know your strengths and weaknesses. If you have a weakness and struggle with it every day to make a living, then you should not choose a free-time activity that reinforces this weakness.

There are, however, exceptions to this rule. If you can visualize long-term benefit from an activity, that prospect can teach you to tolerate it because of the ultimate good it will do. Running, jogging, or doing calisthenics are good examples. You may not like it today but you know it will be good for you. It will improve your body, your appearance, your health.

This is where daily activities dovetail with life planning. When you awake in the morning, you may despise the thought of donning your sweat suit and running, but you know that at the end of the hour it will feel good. Thus, self-control, motivation and long-range improvement can prompt you to persevere in your chosen activity. Also remember that it is not necessary always to use the same activity for creative procrastination.

*How can I use creative procrastination for self-renewal?*

Many people, especially at mid-life, feel stultified and need a change, a new surge of excitement. Sometimes the hours of creative procrastination may be used to turn a hobby into a new avocation or to practice an occupation that once was rejected.

An accountant used his free time to accumulate a set of tools in his garage workshop. As a youth he had liked wood and wanted to be a cabinet maker but turned to accounting because it seemed a more secure occupation. Now he makes beautiful furniture in his spare time.

A young woman who is an artist also likes photography. "Now when I have free time," she said, "I don't have to do something disciplined about my art. Then I can have fun playing and experimenting with the camera." This was her means of self-renewal, using similar talents but not in the way she used them professionally.

*Can creative procrastination be used for meeting a new challenge?*

Definitely yes. Many people miss the element of risk and excitement that is absent from the average job or profession. Some climb mountains, some take up flying, hanggliding, or hot air ballooning. Some shoot the rapids on a white water stream in a rubber boat.

After eight years, a machine repair foreman in an industrial plant felt he had mastered his trade. He had also landscaped the family home and needed a new outlet for his restless energy. Following a youthful dream, he took a second mortgage on his house to buy a racing car and spent his free time on a southwestern U.S. racing circuit.

A more conservative person would consider this foolish economic risk and physically dangerous. Of course it is, but the challenge, putting into action his love for racing vehicles, was what this young man needed. Part of the function of creative procrastination is to give the child within a new opportunity to live and breathe. Most of us submerge our youthful urges in the drive for success and security. Such submergence may be commendable according to standard norms, but life cannot be complete without occasional risk and excitement.

*How do you procrastinate at home?*

Relating the question to evenings after work, the answers most commonly are: "I watch television; I read the newspaper; I play with the kids; I take a nap; I mix a drink and unwind." These activities qualify neither as creative nor negative procrastination. They are not negative because you have earned the free time and feel no guilt about using it. On the other hand, little is accomplished. Some of these activities might be better classified as *passive* or *neutral* procrastination.

One primary criterion for creative procrastination is enjoyment, but is that enough qualification? You may enjoy retiring to your study with the evening paper but your spouse and children may need to be with you during those hours for *their* creative procrastination. During these times you are not entirely free to use your time as you choose. You can reach harmony with yourself only if you act in harmony with the people you love, those who live with you. If you procrastinate privately when they need you, you are negatively selfish. Later on you may decide if this is duty time or if you choose it for relaxation and pleasure. The ideal situation is that you actually like what you must do. Some activities you feel compelled to do with your family can then become creative procrastination.

This does not mean, however, that you must give up all private free time. By communicating clear messages to your family, you can establish the fact that during part of the evening or weekend you will be with them, but the other part will be for you alone.

You may agree that upon alternate evenings your partner will choose which part of the evening you'll share and what you'll do with the time. The important thing is to communicate clearly and assertively so you both understand and accept the ground rules and do not offend each other. A couple also might share a hobby, such as jewelry making or coin collecting, and enjoy their hours of free time together. The same plan can work with children when, for example, a father and son enjoy model building or a sport together. The happier marriages or living combinations are those in which the group members enjoy free time activities together.

*How do I procrastinate creatively at work?*

We have discussed the use of coffee breaks and lunch hours as opportunities for walking, thinking, planning, shopping. It is also possible to take a few minutes between tasks or appointments to meditate and refresh yourself. Executives may have the option of completing their work in the morning and taking an occasional afternoon for golf.

However, the majority of men and women are in work situations where their activity, or lack of it, is observed. Such people are not free to tell a secretary to shut off phone calls so they may meditate.

This type of work, fortunately, is becoming less prevalent as enlightened managers begin thinking less in terms of hours worked and concentrate more on the end result— "management by objective." It may soon be possible to negotiate with your boss in terms of results instead of the eight to five routine, a relatively new idea known as "flex time." Some corporations now contract with employees for production rates rather than standard hours worked. For the effective planner this leaves adequate time for creativity and relaxation.

For those who have not yet attained this sensible situation, there are still ways to procrastinate creatively. No one can see into your mind and no one controls it. You can say to yourself: "All right, that's enough sustained concentration. I'm going to a quiet place in my mind to think of something else, to clear my head and meditate." You can do this even while going through routine motions. Unless supervision is excessively strict, you can also retire to the rest room or away from the work station and take a break. Most managers recognize an employee is more efficient if he or she can enjoy occasional relief from routine. That's why coffee breaks, lunch hours, weekends, and vacations developed in the first place.

*How do I procrastinate if I am a doctor whose day is booked with appointments from 8 A.M. to 10 P.M.?*

Whether or not you are locked into a non-stop schedule is your choice. We have proposed setting aside a one-hour appointment for yourself each day, taking adequate lunch hours, and leaving at least one day free per week while someone else covers your practice.

This question is important because professionals are generally highly motivated to perform their duties and don't take adequate free time from work. The difficulty is not that of finding time, but convincing yourself that time is important to you. Once you make that decision, then free time becomes part of your daily ritual. You don't need a daily dialogue to decide if you will brush your teeth. The same attitude should govern minutes taken for relaxation. This must become an unquestioned act that you choose to do. Consider your own health to be as important as that of any client or patient.

*How do I procrastinate creatively on vacation?*

It may seem redundant to talk about self-indulgence on vacation when the entire time is obstensibly for that purpose, but many people are so involved in work that they cannot relax when they leave it. They have forgotten how to enjoy themselves.

Others choose wrong vacations. Typical is the man who wants to go fishing and camping, expecting his wife to do the cooking and camp chores as she does at home. Another measures the success of a vacation in terms of how many miles he drives. He apparently is challenged by the road map instead of the pleasure of sitting beside a lake or mountain stream viewing majestic scenery. These people feel compelled to kill time and call it a vacation, but they return home tense, jangled, and tired. For them it's a relief to go back to the office and rest.

One couple drove from Iowa to California to visit relatives. The wife wanted to relax along the way, since they had allowed plenty of time for the trip, but her husband was in a hurry to reach their destination. "Do you know," she confided upon their arrival, "we've been fighting all the way from Utah."

It's a common observation that many marriages break up during long rides in closed automobiles. This makes it all the more important to choose the right vacation to help you unwind from workaday routine. Some people like long vacations; others prefer a few days at a time. Some can afford a long unpaid time away from work. Others simply relish a free weekend.

When you plan a vacation, ask: "What is the most relaxing thing we can do?" Take your partner's and children's wishes into consideration because they need to unwind, too. Your family may really like camping and sharing the outdoor chores. Or you all may prefer an ocean cruise or guided tour when someone else serves the food and is responsible for tedious details. True creative procrastination is time that is worry free. Decide for yourself how best to achieve this. It's better to take only a few days, and pay for the privilege of basking in luxury, than to take a long vacation that involves discomfort, tension, and quarreling.

A couple may also decide to take separate vacations, which is one way to solve holiday disagreements. Besides doing exactly what you want to do, the separate vacation also provides a refreshed atmosphere when husband and wife come back together again.

*I work and feel guilty about not spending enough time with my young daughter. What can I do about it?*

There should be no problem if the child is well cared for during the day and if you are consistent in giving undivided love and attention when you are home together. The key is to focus your attention upon work while you are there, and then turn off work, focusing totally upon your child when you are home. You are better off as a part-time good and loving mother, than as a full-time miserable mother.

*The only time I can take time off from work is when I take the kids out to play in the park. Is that creative procrastination?*

It depends on your feelings and attitude. If you enjoy being with the children, then it is creative procrastination. If you do not, it's just another chore. A woman commented that when she wants to take an hour off from a busy day, she likes to play with her baby. This is definitely a creative use of her free time. The mother who does not like to do things with young children—but feels they need it for their development—is doing it as part of her duties. Therefore she deserves some additional time for her own recreation.

*There are so many things to be done that I get confused and overwhelmed; how can I sort them out and catch up with myself?*

The best way is to divide up your tasks into lists labeled *A*, *B*, and *C*. The *A* list contains jobs that are *important* and *urgent*. The *B* lists holds those that are important but not urgent. The *C* list includes items that are neither important nor urgent but must be done sometime.

Let's look at the items which might appear on a typical Saturday list, when you're home from work: Prepare meals and cleanup; clean the house; do the laundry; shop for groceries; water the flowers; and shop for new living room suite. Obviously, this list is more than a heavy load for one day. How can we break it down to *A*, *B*, and *C*? It's as simple as judging each job according to its urgency and importance.

- Cooking and dishwashing: *A* list (every day).

- Clean the house: important, but urgency depends upon the immediate need; it can go on the *B* list today. The same is true with the laundry.
- Shop for groceries: *A* list for a few items but the main shopping can wait.
- Water the flowers: they're newly-planted and will die if not cared for daily. *A* list.
- Shopping for furniture: not critical. *C* list.

So we wind up with only a few items which must be done today. Tackle the highest priority jobs in order. If your *A* list is finished early, you may take some time for creative procrastination or move on to your *B* list, depending upon your energy level. In fact, if you enjoy window shopping, your *C* item might become part of your procrastination.

A similar list for a corporate executive can also be made.

- Labor contract negotiation—*A* list. A strike is threatened.
- Discuss next year's budget—*B* list because time is not yet critical. May move to the *A* list next week.
- Discuss top level promotions—*A* list.
- Meet with potential customers—*A* or *B* list, depending upon importance of the individual.
- Handle correspondence—*C* list except for important items flagged by your secretary.

The *A,B,C* process is simply a matter of setting priorities. This is determined by measuring each task in terms of punishment (if it isn't done) and reward (if it is done). For example, you receive a traffic ticket. If you don't pay the fine within a week, you must appear in court. You know it's important and there is a deadline, so on the final day this duty also becomes urgent. Penalty for failure is the inconvenience of making a court appearance. Likewise, if you put off paying the utility bills, you risk having these vital services discontinued.

Most *B* items on your list will eventually become *A*'s, as their importance and urgency increases. However, *C*-rated tasks seldom progress to the stage of urgency. Almost all duties can be categorized in this way and the sooner you begin doing it, the sooner you will clear away confusion and achieve more free time as a bonus.

*What if a person is overly-organized?*

This usually applies to the person who writes everything on one list and wants to do everything the same day. When he falls short, he transfers the leftovers to the next day, but still on top of the list. Typically he keeps transferring items until the list becomes overwhelming and he is no better off than in the beginning. Perhaps too many *C* items are included in the *A* and *B* lists. Re-evaluate. Is the job really important and urgent? If not, keep it off the *A* list for the day. Keep only a few items on the *A* list and only things which *must* and *can* be done today.

As you set up your priority lists, estimate the amount of time you think each task will require. When done, compare it with the actual time consumed. Many people either over- or under-estimate the time necessary to do a job. Measure how you actually do it and learn for next time.

*I write notes to myself but I lose them, then I waste time looking for the notes.*

Obviously, you are poorly organized. First, don't write notes on scattered scraps of paper. Write your lists in a note book or tablet which is kept near at hand.

There is a possibility, psychologically speaking, that you *want* to lose your notes but are not consciously aware of it. If you are going to assign your work according to priority, you must want to do it. You must be willing to make decisions and follow through. It is not really difficult to decide which jobs are important and urgent. The hard part is doing them in logical order.

*As a salesman, I find it hard to organize the day's activities, to decide in the morning what is most important to do first.*

This is not an uncommon problem for people who must organize work of an unstructured nature. First, you need to be aware of the elements of your work. A part of your day, should be spent in familiarizing yourself with your product line and how this fits the needs of the potential customer. A salesman's first impulse in the morning might be to start making client calls. Before he does so, however, he should learn everything possible about the client as well as the best communications approach.

Once he is aware of the necessary preparations, he should be able to organize his day, taking into account his own natural rhythms. He may be more alert in the morning or afternoon and should schedule his calls accordingly. One salesman, after a study of his biological rhythms, discovered that his high and low periods fluctuated on a 48-hour cycle. Once he recognized this, he was able to schedule client calls on his "up" days and spent his "off" days taking care of required paper work.

*I'm a supervisor and I like answering questions. However, people often linger to socialize after everything has been said. I get irritated because they're using my time, but what can I do to turn them off without hurting their feelings?*

Learn to be politely assertive. You need sentences ready to use without guilt on people who really impose on you. Your role is to convey information, not to serve as mother or supporter. Taking time to advise people is legitimate, but it is not legitimate when they try to use you.

*I have trouble getting back to work after a weekend or vacation, or I find it easy getting to work but have trouble unwinding when I leave it.*

The answer is essentially the same for both questions: provide some *overlap* time. If you're going away for the weekend, and it's hard to get into a relaxed mood, start thinking about pleasant aspects of the trip before the end of the day on Friday. If you have trouble getting back into the work routine, start thinking about it Sunday night: what do I need for work tomorrow; what is the first task that will confront me; and do I have all the materials I will need? Then plan the first half of Monday in detail so that you start with clear expectations and motivation.

*What if I set too many short-term goals? How can I tell if they are realistic?*

The test of a short-term goal is whether or not it fits with your long-term goals. If you want to go to school and finish in a year's time, then you know you must study so many hours every day to achieve the goal. If you study just for fun without any specific final goal, then you might ask: "Why do I study so much every day when I want to do other things?" Realism in setting goals must also include measuring how much you *can* do in a day or week. Your stamina plays a part in the decision. Sometimes you have more energy and can do more, at other times less. If you cannot plan your day at your best pace, including time for creative procrastination, then your goals are not realistic and something must give.

*How can creative procrastination improve my health?*

By respecting your physical, mental and emotional needs and scheduling free time to cater to them.

## The New Contract

The following points, practiced regularly, will become your action plan to better living. *Write it into the form of a contract with yourself, sign it, and review it periodically to reinforce your self-discipline.*

1. I commit myself to redefine procrastination. If done creatively, it's okay and it's my choice.
2. At home I will combine my creative procrastination needs with those of my family so that we will live in harmony.
3. We will choose vacations to fit our budget but also to gain a change of pace and routine that will help us unwind and relax.
4. I will find new ways to cope with stress and challenge at work.
5. In the past year I have not exercised enough and my body suffers. I commit myself to the following (list the activities along with how and when you will do them).
6. In the past year I have not taken enough time for recreation. I commit myself to (list your plan for recreation along with specific times and places).
7. I will change my nutrition habits and control my weight (write down how you plan to do this).
8. I will use _____ method of relaxation (be specific).
9. I will control my degenerative habits (such as smoking, drinking, and poor sleep patterns).

If you make this nine-point commitment, and keep it, you will feel enriched, both in health and in achievements. The integration of whole body health routines with creative procrastination will give you higher self-esteem, and the feeling that you're really in charge of your life and your potential for power, success, and good health.

These are the rewards for managing your time creatively.

# Bibliography

Alberti, Robert E., and Emmons, Michael L. *Your Perfect Right.* San Luis Obispo, Calif.: Impact Press, 1970.

Ardell, Donald B. *High Level Wellness: An Alternative to Doctors, Drugs and Disease.* Emmaus, Pa.: Rodale Press, 1977.

Barrett, F. D. "The Management of Time." *The Business Quarterly,* Spring (1960), pp. 56–66.

Bennett, Arnold. *How to Live on 24 Hours a Day.* New York: Cornerstone Library, 1966.

Benson, Herbert, M.D. and Klipper, Miriam Z., *The Relaxation Response.* New York: Avon Books, 1975.

Bittel, Lester R. *The Nine Master Keys to Management.* McGraw-Hill, New York: 1972.

Brooks, Earl. "Get More Done—Easier," *Nations Business,* July (1962), pp. 254–256.

Brown, Barbara B. *Stress and the Art of Biofeedback.* New York: Bantam Books, 1977.

Cooper, Joseph D. *How to Get More Done in Less Time.* Garden City, New York: Doubleday, 1971.

de Grazia, Sebastian. *Of Time, Work and Leisure.* New York: Doubleday, 1962.

Drucker, Peter F. *The Effective Executive.* New York: Harper & Row, 1967.

Ellis, Albert, and Knaus, William J. *Overcoming Procrastination.* New York: Institute for Rational Living, 1977.

Ellul, Jacques. *The Technological Society.* New York: Alfred A. Knopf, 1964.

Engstrom, Ted W., and Mackenzie, R. Alec. *Managing Your Time: Practical Guidelines on the Effective Use of Time.* Grand Rapids: Zondervan Publishing House, 1967.

Flory, Charles D., ed. *Managers for Tomorrow.* New York: New American Library, 1965.

Hennig, Margaret and Jardim, Anne. *The Managerial Woman.* Garden City, N.Y.: Anchor Press, 1977.

Heyel, Carl. *Organizing Your Job in Management.* New York: American Management Association., 1960.

Jennings, Eugene E. *The Executive in Crisis.* New York: McGraw-Hill, 1965.

Jones, Curtis H. "The Money Value of Time," *Harvard Business Review,* July–August (1968), pp. 94–101.

Lakein, Alan. *How to Get Control of Your Time and Your Life.* New York: Peter H. Wyden, Inc., 1973.

Levinson, Harry. *Executive Stress.* New York: New American Library, 1964.

Mackenzie, R. Alec. *The Time Trap.* New York: American Management Association, 1972.

———. *New Time Management Methods for You and Your Staff.* Chicago: The Dartnell Corp., 1975.

McCay, James T. *The Management of Time.* (Prentice-Hall, Englewood Cliffs, N.J.: Prentice-Hall, 1959.

McQuade, Walter, and Aikman, Ann. *Stress.* New York: Bantam Books, 1974.

Meininger, Jut. *Success Through Transactional Analysis.* New York: Signet, 1973.

Moore, Leo B. "Managerial Time," *Indiana Management Review,* Spring (1968), pp. 77–85.

Moskowitz, Robert. *Total Time Management.* AMACOM, a division of the American Management Ass'n., 1975.

Oates, Wayne E. *Workaholics, Make Laziness Work for You.* New York: Doubleday, 1978.

Oyle, Dr. Irving. *The Healing Mind: You Can Cure Yourself Without Drugs.* Millbrae, Calif.: Celestial Arts, 1975.

Parkinson, C. Northcote. *Parkinson's Law.* Boston: Houghton Mifflin, 1957.

Peter, Laurence J. and Hull, Raymond. *The Peter Principle.* New York: Bantam Books, 1971.

Porat, Frieda, and Quackenbush, Margery. *Positive Selfishness.* Millbrae, California: Celestial Arts, 1977.

Selye, Hans. *Stress Without Distress.* New York: New American Library, 1974.

Trickett, Joseph M. "A More Effective Use of Time," *California Management Review,* Summer 1962.

Webber, Ross A. *Time and Management.* New York: Van Nostrand Reinhold, 1972.